15 Things You Should Give Up to Be Happy

15 Things
You Should
Give Up to
Be Happy

An Inspiring Guide to
Discovering Effortless Joy

Luminita D. Saviuc

A PERIGEE BOOK

To Danny and Lecsy

P

PERIGEE
An imprint of Penguin Random House LLC
375 Hudson Street, New York, New York 10014

LIBRARY OF CONGRESS CATALOGING-IN-PUBLICATION DATA
Saviuc, Luminita D., author.
15 things you should give up to be happy : an inspiring guide to discovering effortless joy / Luminita D. Saviuc ; foreword by Vishen Lakhiani. — First edition.
pages cm
ISBN 978-0-399-17282-3 (paperback)
1. Happiness. 2. Conduct of life. I. Title. II. Title: Fifteen things you should give up to be happy.
BJ1481.S325 2016
152.4'2—dc23   2015032168

First edition: March 2016

PRINTED IN THE UNITED STATES OF AMERICA

5   7   9   10   8   6   4

Text design by Elke Sigal

Most Perigee books are available at special quantity discounts for bulk purchases for sales promotions, premiums, fund-raising, or educational use. Special books, or book excerpts, can also be created to fit specific needs. For details, write: SpecialMarkets@ penguinrandomhouse.com.

CONTENTS

CONTENTS

FOREWORD

When I first met Luminita, she had just arrived in Malaysia for a career change, to begin a new role with my education company, Mindvalley. I never could have guessed just what an impact she would soon have on my learning and growth, and on the millions of lives she would later touch through her writing.

I didn't realize then that she is a powerhouse—a powerhouse who overcame painful and traumatic circumstances, yet emerged a beacon of light.

Even in those early days, though, the signs were evident. It was clear to everyone how much she genuinely cared about helping people. Luminita often received amazing words of gratitude from our students for her thoughtful and comforting responses. For an organization that primarily focuses on empowering others with transformational education, this was a valuable trait. But that was only the beginning.

One of the things I will always admire about Luminita is how avid a student she is. Often, on her breaks in the office, I'd see her studying the work of authors such as Wayne Dyer, Lao Tzu, and Louise Hay, just to name a few, then later sharing what she had learned with others around her, and through her blog, in deceptively simple yet powerful ways that uplifted them, and changed their lives.

At one point she even started a coaching group at Mindvalley, drawing wisdom from the Tao Te Ching. As if expanding our minds was not enough, she then got us on an exercise plan, inspiring her friends and colleagues, including me, to give up some of the mindsets and habits that were stopping us from being healthier and more joyful. I never thought I'd have the discipline to commit to a thirty-day intensive exercise regimen, but I did, because Luminita had the power to persuade, prod and move us to just do it.

And that's precisely what this heartfelt book will help you with, too. Based on her famous blog post "15 Things You Should Give Up To Be Happy," which went viral and was shared on Facebook more than 1.2 million times, it will inspire you and help you to transform your life from the inside out.

Peppered with personal stories, quotes, and powerful insights that have inspired millions, this book reveals how Luminita, despite her abusive childhood, persevered and believed in her growth and her healing, and how you can, too.

In the chapters that follow, you will learn about the wisdom of giving yourself permission to give up—that is, to let go of what holds you back. You will discover how to give up the past, the need to always be right, blaming others, and much, much more. At each step along the way Luminita will invite you, through parables, personal stories, and uplifting words, to truly take hold of your life by simply letting go.

Anyone who has lived through what Luminita did and managed to emerge with such remarkable inner strength, to become the luminous being that she is, is someone for whom I have profound respect, and someone we can all learn from.

And so, I encourage you to dive into *15 Things You Should*

Give Up to Be Happy, and be truly inspired by the hard-won lessons of someone who has managed to turn her life around, let go of the past, and heal herself so that she could seek her ultimate truth—to live at the peak of her human potential and inspire the lives of many others. I hope you'll take great insight from Luminita's work, as I have.

Vishen Lakhiani
Founder and CEO, Mindvalley

INTRODUCTION

It was a peaceful and quiet night in our home. The kind you don't want to remember. It was cold, and the sky was dark. As dark as the memories of those years.

My siblings and I were sitting in the middle of our living room, watching TV while my parents were somewhere in the house.

As we were sitting there, enjoying ourselves, we suddenly heard our father's angry screaming voice, breaking the stillness.

"Who took them?!"

"There are candies missing, who took them?!"

"Who ate the candies?!"

Without saying a single word, I looked at one of my sisters, and from the look on her face I immediately knew she was the one who took them.

She looked horrified. We all did. Tears were running down our faces. We were all scared because we knew what was about to happen.

He then asked again, this time with an even angrier voice:

"Who took the damn candies? Answer me!"

Nobody dared to say a word.

"Who took them?!"

"If the person who took the candies won't admit it, you will all get in big trouble! All of you, you hear me?! All of you!"

Without waiting for my father to ask the question one more time, with tears pouring down my face, I replied:

"I took them. I took the candies. It was me."

I am not sure why exactly I decided to take on the blame, but I did. Maybe it was because I knew I could live with my pain but not with somebody else's pain. I just didn't want him to hurt my sister.

"I am sorry. I ate them. I ate them all. Please forgive me. Please!"

The moment I said it was me, he pulled me by my hair and started dragging me all the way to the bathroom.

I wasn't even ten years old at that time, and I remember crying and screaming so loudly, begging him to let go of my hair, begging him for forgiveness.

"Please, Father, please. Let me go. I'm sorry. I'm sorry. I won't do it again."

He was silent, and it felt like he couldn't hear a word I was saying.

He threw me on the bathroom floor and started screaming:

"Bring me the gasoline! Bring me the gasoline!"

"You will see what happens to those who steal from me! You will see what you get for lying to me! Just wait and see!"

I was so terrified, not knowing what he wanted the gasoline for.

My father used to do many strange things, and one of them was to bring gasoline into our apartment. In the middle of our living room, we had this gigantic box filled with bottles of gasoline. There were more than one hundred liters of gasoline in our home.

"Bring me the gasoline! Bring me the gasoline or I will burn you all.

Now!"

After he finished inserting paper between my toes, he began pouring gasoline on my toes and eventually lit me on fire.

I was horrified.

"Please, Father, please! I won't do it again. Please stop! Please!"

Tears ran down my face and warmed my cheeks like never before, as the smell of smoke filled the air around my nostrils.

"It hurts, it hurts! Please help me! Please! Somebody please help me. Please . . ."

I was in so much pain, screaming and begging him to put out the fire, praying to God that my father would eventually feel sorry for me and stop.

Every second that fire was burning felt like an eternity to me. I really thought I wouldn't make it out alive.

I am not sure how long I stood there with my toes on fire, but I do know that at one point I passed out.

I felt drained, exhausted. I couldn't fight anymore and my body collapsed.

I wasn't even taken to the hospital. It was my mom and my siblings who took care of me as best as they could, making sure I was safe.

After that incident, I couldn't walk properly for months because my toes were damaged.

I remember my teachers and the kids at school asking me:

"Luminita, what is wrong with your feet? Why are you walking like this? Are you okay? What happened?"

To which, with a smile on my face, I would reply:

"Nothing. Nothing is wrong. I am okay. I am fine."

But I wasn't. Oh no, I wasn't.

· · ·

You may be wondering why I started a book on happiness with this story from my childhood. Here is my answer to you, my reader.

For more than five years, as a blogger, as the author behind PurposeFairy, and before starting to write this book, I received many criticisms and comments from people who felt that my ideas and tips for being happy in life were naive at best, and dangerously stupid at worst.

They felt like the ideas, tips, tools and recommendations I wrote about and offered didn't apply to them and couldn't help them. They proclaimed that they would only work on people who grew up "normal." They argued that the stories and insights you hold within your hands right now, in these pages, didn't have the power to positively transform people who had gone through horrible and traumatic experiences.

Well, I am here to tell you that what I have to share with you has worked for me. I say this as someone who:

> Lived with an alcoholic and abusive father for more than twelve years.
> Got deprived of love and nourishment throughout her entire childhood.
> Used to believe that your self-worth came from your net worth and, since she never had enough of the latter, suffered from low self-esteem.
> Got abused physically, mentally and emotionally for years and years.

Lived in crappy, crowded orphanages with mean,
    irresponsible caretakers.

Got ridiculed, labeled, judged and laughed at
    constantly all throughout her childhood and
    teenage years.

Struggled with giving up on, and letting go of, the
    person she loved the most, her former longtime
    boyfriend.

And much, much more.

I don't say this because I want or need your sympathy (I don't). I share it to elaborate the extent of the horrible things that I had to go through and to make a simple point: The story of your past doesn't have to become the story of your life. Your past does not have to be your future.

> *The story of your past doesn't have to become the story of your life.*

Not only that, but you can also go on to have a happy life full of beauty, joy and fulfillment.

It's absolutely possible, and in this book I share the lessons of that journey along with insights from ancient Eastern wisdom, contemporary spirituality and scientific research in positive psychology—all things which have been tremendously helpful to me and helped me with my healing.

It all worked for me. More importantly, it worked for many of my friends and thousands upon thousands of people who have read my blog. Therefore I suspect it might also work for you.

What you're about to read is based on a post on my blog entitled "15 Things You Should Give Up to Be Happy," which was shared on Facebook more than 1.2 million times. This book is an in-depth elaboration of everything I wrote about in that post, so you can gain the benefits of more details, examples and ideas, considered and explored from different angles and viewpoints.

Can I promise you 100 percent that everything in the book will work for you? No, I can't promise that, but based on what I have seen and witnessed I do believe that its message will help you live a happier and better life.

It includes stories about my first horrible heartbreak, how I traveled from one country to another, leaving everything behind me, getting lost in order to be found, and how I managed to go from living a sad and hopeless life filled with drama and negativity to becoming the person that I am today: liberated, financially independent, self-expressed and free to travel the world to enjoy beautiful locations, from Miami Beach to Bali's temples and rice fields. I've also included a few stories from readers who have reached out to me, sharing their own struggles and triumphs. I hope they will inspire you, as they have inspired me.

In a world where we are led to believe that happiness, wealth and success come from being better than everyone else, or having, doing and knowing more, this book comes to prove the exact opposite.

It is in giving up that we find happiness, our way back home and life's missing pieces. So without further ado, I say, give up and be happy. Let's begin.

It is in giving up that we find happiness, our way back home and life's missing pieces.

Chapter 1

GIVE UP THE PAST

One problem with gazing too frequently into the past is that we may turn around to find the future has run out on us.

—MICHAEL CIBENKO

MY STORY

Throughout the late 1980s and early 1990s, life for my family and me, in our European home country of Romania, which was transitioning out of Communism at the time, was far from pleasant.

For years, my mom and my siblings were as terrified of my father as I was. So much so that I used to huddle under my blanket, on a small pillow, and with tears in my eyes pray to God to keep me and my family safe.

However, life was very hard, not only at home but everywhere I went.

Kids at school and on the playground were taking turns making fun of me and calling me hurtful names; teachers were looking down on me, giving me the pity look, treating me as if I were less valuable than the other kids in my class; our neighbors were throwing harsh words at me and my siblings, telling us how tired they were of us living in the same building with them and that they wanted us out. Everywhere I went, people seemed to have something against me and my family.

As time went by, I began to think that maybe they were right to treat me so poorly and that maybe I was less valuable than most people.

As a result I began using all kinds of negative, toxic and self-defeating words to describe myself and my life. I grew up thinking I wasn't a worthy human being. I grew up thinking I wasn't worthy to be happy, respected and loved. I grew up thinking I was small and insignificant and that I would never be anything else but the girl who came from a "dysfunctional" family and who was now doomed to repeat the same mistakes her parents made and to live a sad and unhappy life.

Then suddenly, after I turned twelve, my father died.

. . .

The power of the past is a strange one. Despite my father's death, I carried my first twelve years with me wherever I went, allowing the burdens of those times to weigh me down and to keep me feeling trapped, stuck and unhappy.

Because I didn't know how to release the pain that my father inflicted upon me; because I didn't know how to accept, embrace, forgive, release and let go of all those past hurts, I continued to allow the past to define me and my life. I continued to suffer.

Worse, if for the first twelve years of my life my father had been my bully, after his death it was almost as if I decided to take his place and become my own bully. I became my own worst enemy.

I started abusing myself and despising my mom, neighbors, teachers and many of the bullies in school and on the playground.

I even got to a point where I couldn't stand to look at myself in the mirror, I was so lacking in self-love, self-confidence and self-respect.

"Why did you have to drag us through all this mess?" I often yelled at my mother, making sure she knew what a horrible parent I thought she was.

"Why didn't you leave Father years ago?"

"Why did we have to suffer because of your mistakes?"

"It's because of you that we are as messed up as we are!"

"It's all your fault!"

"I will never have a normal life because of you!"

"It's all your fault, Mom . . ."

"I hate you so god damn much!"

I wanted people to acknowledge me and my pain. I wanted them to understand what I was going through and to come to my "rescue." But nobody ever did. Nobody.

LESSONS IN LETTING GO

You are not a victim. No matter what you have been through, you're still here. You may have been challenged, hurt, betrayed, beaten, and discouraged, but nothing has defeated you. You are still here! You have been delayed but not denied. You are not a victim, you are a victor. You have a history of victory.

—STEVE MARABOLI

I used to think I was a victim of my past. I used to think that just because I was born and raised in a very unhappy and violent environment, I was doomed to live that way for the rest of my life.

Well, guess what? I was wrong.

The moment you decide that you have had enough of everything, enough of stress and anxiety, enough of anger and resentment, enough of struggle, lack, pain and poverty, enough of tears, heartbreaks, self-destructive thoughts, behaviors and relationships and enough of all that is negative and toxic, that will be the moment you will finally be ready to take charge of your life and take the necessary steps toward a better and happier life.

· · ·

It took me a long time to realize that the only salvation I ever needed was from my own toxic thoughts and from my own self. The moment I realized this truth, I was able to finally open my eyes and see things clearly for the first time in my life.

I remember thinking to myself:

Yes, you were a victim when your father was alive. You were young and couldn't defend yourself. Once he was gone, the gate to your "prison cell" was opened. You were free to escape and live a happy life. Free from the past and free to build a new life for yourself. But your attachment to all those past hurts kept you inside the "prison cell" your father placed you in the first twelve years of your life, made you believe that you were still a victim of your past and that you would continue to be trapped in the past for the rest of your life.

> If there must be madness, chaos and time crunches in your life, then let there be chaos. These things are happening around you; nothing is happening to you. Find the strength and stillness to be the eye inside that storm.
>
> —AMY JIRSA

It's not easy to go from perceiving yourself as a victim to deciding that you have the power to do something about your life, you have the power to change things around. It's not easy to accept the pain that you harbor and work on accepting, forgiving and giving up on your past.

It's not easy to accept the fact that people mistreated you and treated you unkindly in the past and that you were deprived of love, happiness and affection.

It's not easy to make peace with your past hurts, surrender

and let go of it all, but if you do it, your life will be forever transformed and good things will start happening to you, because of you.

Your past doesn't have to equal your future, unless you want it to.

Your past doesn't have to equal your future, unless you want it to.

Ivone, one of my blog readers, understands this truth deeply. After having lost her beloved parents three years ago, she was able to overcome that sense of loss with the help of her loving fiancé, who had always supported her, and gave her the strength she needed to move forward. When she lost him as well, in a car accident, Ivone completely shut down. She felt heartbroken, angry, frustrated and disappointed at God and the whole world because she just couldn't understand why this was happening to her.

It felt so unfair to be so unhappy and see everyone else go on with their lives as if nothing was wrong. As a result, Ivone became bitter and resentful and started pushing everyone away, including herself. She gave up on her will to live, she gave up on herself, and she gave up on the hope that she was ever going to be happy again. After a while, seeing that she was going down a path of self-destruction, she decided to let it all go—to let go of the pain she was harboring in her heart, to let go of the bitterness and resentment that was poisoning her mind, her relationships and her life, and to accept what had happened. When she did so, not only did she manage to free herself of the heavy burden of the past, she also found the inner strength to make peace with the idea that things don't always happen the way we expect them to happen, and that's okay. Now she's living a peaceful, harmonious life, expressing her gratitude on a daily basis for every experience life sends her way, good or bad.

If you cling to the past and keep on using it as an excuse for not moving on with your life, then yes, your future will be very similar to your past. On the other hand, if you give up the past and allow yourself to be present and engaged in your day-to-day life, while at the same time having a clear vision of what you want your future to look like, then your future will be nothing like your past. It's all up to you. You have the power to decide. The future of your life is in your hands.

.　.　.

Isn't it ironic how we use something as precious as the present moment to fill with past hurts? We think and talk about the past, we think and talk about the future, but we rarely stop to pay attention to the present moment.

We don't cling to the past because we want to suffer, but because we think that by holding on to it we will be happy. This is the irony.

We cling to the past because the past gives us a sense of identity; it makes us who we are, or at least that's what we think. Because we haven't yet learned how to be present and engaged in our day-to-day lives, we continue to craft our lives from a place of limitations—the past—instead of doing it from a place of infinite choices and possibilities—the present moment.

Thank goodness, we have a choice.

THE PATH TO "GIVING UP"

1. Commitment

When one door of happiness closes, another opens; but often we look so long at the closed door that we do not see the one which has been opened for us.

—HELEN KELLER

Make a commitment to yourself:

I (your name),
Make a commitment to myself to work on letting go of what's behind me and start appreciating what's in front of me.
I accept and appreciate the past for all the lessons it had to teach me, and I allow my past experiences to make me a better not a bitter person.
I will work on disciplining my mind to be present and engaged in the now, and I promise myself to make the best

*out of every experience life sends my way, either good
or bad.*

*I promise myself to become a source of inspiration for
myself and those around me and to spread love and
positivity wherever I go.*

*I promise myself to live life fully and to always be
honest with myself, even at the risk of "offending" those
around me.*

*I give myself permission to forgive, to love and to be
thankful for every experience life sends my way.*

*I give myself permission to turn my wounds into
wisdom and my difficulties into opportunities.*

*I give myself permission to love myself, the people
around me and my life.*

*I give myself permission to make the rest of my life the
best of my life.*

Sincerely,

(Your name)

. . .

Because of the many years of our past conditioning and the intense training we have in holding on to things, letting go won't
happen overnight, and that's okay. Be patient and gentle with
yourself while working on this process and remember to take
one step at a time. A journey of a thousand miles begins with
a single step after all.

There is plenty of happiness waiting for you in your present life, and all you have to do is make a commitment to yourself to give up the past and start enjoying the present moment.

Once you commit to making it happen, nothing and no one will be able to stand between you and your happiness.

2. Acceptance

> What often screws us up the most in life is the picture
> in our head of how it's supposed to be.
> —UNKNOWN

The moment you become attached to how things should be, how people and life should treat you and how your happiness should be packaged and delivered your way, you create a lot of resistance and unhappiness in your life.

Let go of this image you have in your head of how life should have been or how it should be. Discipline your mind to work with you not against you, to lift you up and not to tear you down.

If your past was painful and traumatic, work on healing the wounds that were created. Accept your struggles, your so-called failures and mistakes, your wounds and past hurts. Accept it all. Don't resist it.

On the other hand, if your past was a glorious and happy one and your present life is far from matching that perfect picture, instead of being bitter and resentful toward your present reality, work on using the same mentality, the same tools and the same principles you used in the past to craft a better life and to reinvent yourself. It can be done, and the proof is your past.

Surrender to what is. Accept the past the way it is, with both the good and the bad. Because only by accepting what happened will you be able to leave it all behind and work on crafting a brand-new life for yourself.

Be willing to work on healing any wounds you might have and let go of any anger and resentment you are holding on to. Give yourself permission to work on forgiving those who might have hurt you in the past and to make room in your mind, body and heart for love, peace and tranquility.

Work on accepting, embracing and forgiving it all, no matter how hard and impossible it might seem. Don't cling to the pain, and what's most important, don't let your past define and limit you. Accept your past for what it was and accept your life for what it is now. Only by doing so will you have the power to change your present life situation.

3. Forgiveness

Forgiveness is the most powerful thing that you can do for your physiology and your spirituality. Yet, it remains one of the least attractive things to us, largely because our egos rule so unequivocally. To forgive is somehow associated with saying that it is all right, that we accept the evil deed. But this is not forgiveness. Forgiveness means that you fill yourself with love and you radiate that love outward and refuse to hang onto the venom or hatred that was engendered by the behaviors that caused the wounds.

—WAYNE DYER

A lot of people think that the moment you decide to forgive someone who once hurt you, the person who receives the forgiveness is the only one benefiting from your kind and charitable gesture, but that's not the case. I can tell you for sure that the person who will benefit the most is the person who does the forgiving.

Don't let your mind trick you into thinking that forgiveness is an act of weakness. Contrary to what you have been led to believe, forgiveness is an act of strength.

Forgiveness is an act of strength.

Forgiveness is a gift you give to yourself, to be at peace, to be happy and to be able to sleep at night. You don't forgive because you are weak but because you are strong enough to realize that only by giving up on resentment will you be happy.

If you hold on to poisonous thoughts like hate, anger and resentment toward someone, you will end up poisoning yourself more than you poison the other person, and you will be very unhappy.

. . .

If others mistreated you in the past, it doesn't mean you have to continue their work. Look how beautifully Mark Twain talks about this: "Anger is an acid that can do more harm to the vessel in which it is stored than to anything on which it is poured."

Let go of all the anger, all the toxicity and all the resentment that is poisoning your mind, body, soul and life. If you're mad, be mad. Don't hide and suppress your feelings. Let it all out, and once you're done with being mad, allow forgiveness to enter your heart.

Only by removing all the toxicity from your life will you be able to free yourself from the self-made prison you have been living in for so long.

Fill your heart with love. Forgive and let go. Not necessarily because those who mistreated you deserve it, but because you do. Let forgiveness liberate you from your past. Allow it to take away all the resentment you've kept in your heart for all this time and allow it to fill in that empty space with love.

Forgive, release and let go.

Start small and trust that as you work on letting go of all the extra baggage that is weighing you down, you will start to feel lighter and you will gain a lot more clarity about your life. You will feel happier and more at peace with yourself and the world around you.

I personally had a lot of forgiving to do, especially when it came to my father. But the older I got and the more challenges I had to face on my own, the easier it became for me to understand that, in the words of Thich Nhat Hanh, "When another person makes you suffer, it is because he suffers deeply within himself, and his suffering is spilling over. He does not need punishment; he needs help. That's the message he is sending."

It was forgiveness that helped turn my wounds into wisdom and my anger, bitterness and resentment into love and compassion.

4. Look for the Lessons

And once the storm is over, you won't remember how you made it through, how you managed to survive. You won't even be sure, whether the storm is really over. But one thing is certain. When you come out of the storm, you won't be the same person who walked in. That's what this storm's all about.

—HARUKI MURAKAMI

Don't look for faults. Look for the lessons in everything that has happened to you. Look for the good in the bad, look for the beautiful in the ugly. Being positive and having a grateful attitude will help you cope with life's challenges in a healthier and more empowering way.

Be an alchemist.

Follow Kurt Vonnegut's advice and learn to "Be soft. Do not let the world make you hard. Do not let pain make you hate. Do not let the bitterness steal your sweetness. Take pride that even though the rest of the world may disagree, you still believe it to be a beautiful place."

Take the best out of every experience. Allow your challenges to make you better not bitter. Turn your wounds into wisdom and your difficulties into opportunities. Search for the lessons. Look for the empowering meaning in everything, and when you do so no experience will ever be wasted.

Be a light unto this world. Make light where there was once darkness. Give love to those who have none.

Work on treating everyone with love and compassion, and look to see every person that comes into your life as both your student and your teacher.

Learn from every life experience. Learn from every person. Know that they all have something to teach you.

5. Be Thankful

Be thankful for the bad things in life. For they open your eyes to the good things you weren't paying attention to before.

—UNKNOWN

Shift your focus from the bad onto the good, from the pain onto the gain, from resentment onto forgiveness, gratitude and appreciation. Learn to let go of any regrets and resentment you might be holding on to and look back at your life with thankfulness.

Be thankful to those who mistreated you, for they have showed you how not to live your life.

Be thankful to those who betrayed you. It is because of them that you have learned the power that comes from the act of forgiveness.

Be thankful to those who refused to help you in times of need. It is because of them you have learned how to do it all by yourself.

Be thankful for the difficult times, for they have showed you how strong you can be.

Be thankful for those who labeled, judged and criticized you harshly. It is because of them you have learned that your value and self-worth come from yourself and not from others.

Be thankful to those who gave you no love. It is because of them that you have learned to look for love and approval within yourself.

Be thankful for the many limits that were imposed on you. It is because of them you have learned to break free from all the past conditioning and create your own reality and your own rules.

Be thankful for your past mistakes and failures. It is because of them that you have learned how not to do things. It is because of them that you have learned what works and what doesn't.

Be thankful for both the good and bad experiences life has sent your way. It is because of these experiences that you have learned some of life's most valuable lessons.

Fill your heart with gratitude, appreciation and thankfulness and know that a thankful heart is better than a bitter one.

The moment you start appreciating life exactly as it is, life will start appreciating you exactly as you are.

Chapter 2

GIVE UP YOUR FEARS

Don't give in to your fears. If you do, you won't be able to talk to your heart.

—PAULO COELHO

MY STORY

Since early on, I lived a life governed by fear.

I don't remember exactly how every one of my fears was born, but what I do remember very well is how my fear of abandonment came to be.

I was four or five years old. It was nighttime, and I remember waking up to go to the restroom. I opened my eyes, and wanting to get out of bed, I realized that I couldn't do it because the bed's grilled bars were stopping me. That got me confused simply because we didn't have any grilled beds in our home. Thinking that maybe I was still asleep and probably dreaming, I pinched myself, looked around and realized that nothing had changed. I was still in the same place.

"This isn't a dream . . . I'm not dreaming," I told myself with a soft yet shaky voice.

I was very confused, so I started looking around me. As I was becoming more and more aware of what was happening and where I was, I started feeling very afraid.

"What's going on?"

My heart was now beating very fast.

"Where am I?"

My whole body began to shake, and I could feel the bed moving underneath me, making subtle squeaky noises. The air felt heavier and harder to breathe in what began to feel like a stuffy place.

"Where's my mommy?"

"Why am I here?"

"Who brought me here?"

I couldn't stop myself from shaking. I wanted to make it stop but I found it impossible to control myself.

"Orphanage . . . I'm in an orphanage . . ."

I recognized what an orphanage roughly looked like from a cartoon I used to watch when I was at home. The sight of nearby rows of other similar-looking beds shattered any remaining hope that I could be mistaken.

"It's an orphanage!" The shock had set in, and my eyes welled up with tears yet again like they had a thousand times before throughout my short existence, only worse, and profusely.

"Why am I here?!" I started screaming. The moment those

words came out of my mouth, I felt the temperature in my body drop, as if I were falling through broken ice sheets in the middle of a frozen lake and into the freezing water below.

"Get me out of here!" I screamed out.

Too many questions raced through my mind, so intensely that I don't remember what exactly happened around me as others who were there awakened to my shouting.

"Why am I in an orphanage when my parents are still alive?!"

"Did they abandon me?!"

"Did I do something wrong?!"

"Why am I here?"

"Where is my mommy?"

"Somebody, please take me home!"

"Please, take me back home!"

"Get me out of here!"

"Please ..."

My heart ripped into a million pieces.

LESSONS IN LETTING GO

Tell your heart that the fear of suffering is worse than the suffering itself. And that no heart has ever suffered when it goes in search of its dreams, because every second of the search is a second's encounter with God and with eternity.

—PAULO COELHO

Growing up, I was afraid of everything and everyone—afraid of myself, afraid of the people around me and afraid of life itself. I was suspicious of anyone who dared to show any sign of affection toward me, and for a very long time I felt that I couldn't trust anyone, not even myself. I remember how, whenever anyone would act in a kind and loving way toward me, I would immediately push them away, thinking that if I opened my heart to them, they would eventually hurt, betray and abandon me, just like my parents had that night.

This is what living in fear does to you. Fear makes you doubt the goodness in people. It makes you feel small and insignificant, bitter and resentful, unworthy of anything good. It makes you doubt yourself and everyone around you. It makes you question your own beauty and perfection, and it makes you question the existence of the most beautiful and most real feeling in the world, LOVE. And that's exactly what fear did to me.

.　.　.

For as long as I can remember I wanted to have friends, many friends, but my fear of rejection kept me from making too many of them.

I wanted to laugh, to play and to enjoy the many gifts that life had to offer, but my fear of change kept me from taking the necessary steps that were meant to move me in that direction.

I wanted to have a healthy, loving and supportive relationship, to love and be loved, but my fear of intimacy and my fear of abandonment caused me to sabotage the relationship I had with the person I loved the most, my former longtime boyfriend.

I wanted to experience life fully, to be present and engaged in everything that was happening to me and all around me, to be happy and feel fully alive, but my fear of what had happened in the past, of what might happen in the present or what could happen in the future kept me from doing all of those things.

I wanted to go to a good university, to continue to study art, to use my gifts and talents, to infuse love, beauty and passion into all of my work, but my fear of failure and my fear of not being good enough kept me from doing all of these things.

I wanted happiness, I wanted love, and I wanted to experience the beauty of life, but by constantly nurturing fearful thoughts and by expecting the worst to always happen, I was pushing all those beautiful things away from me.

* * *

The reason why you don't put your hand in the fire is not because of fear, it's because you know you'll get burned. You don't need fear to avoid an unnecessary danger, just a minimum of intelligence and common sense.

—ECKHART TOLLE

If when my father was alive most of my fears were instinctual (an instinctual fear is your body's natural response to real potential harm and danger, when something or someone presents a direct threat to your physical body), in the years that followed his death, all kinds of psychological fears began to surface (a psychological fear is nothing but a creation of your imagination, presenting no real and direct physical threat to you), illusory fears that were meant to give birth to more stress, unhappiness and anxiety, emotions I was so accustomed to.

It took me a very long time to finally understand that you can't hold on to fear and expect to feel loved. You can't hold on to fear and expect to be happy. You can't hold on to fear and expect to receive many of the gifts that life has to offer. It took me a very long time to be able to understand the difference between rational and irrational fears, but once I did, once I understood that many of the things I was so frightened of were only in my head, I immediately started letting go of fear, replacing it with love—love for myself, love for my life and love for the world around me.

> *You can't hold on to fear and*
> *expect to feel loved.*

Whether your fears go back to your earliest memories, as mine did, or they are more recent, unwelcome guests in your life, such as a nagging concern or anxiety about a loved one, or a phobia that has crept into your mind and taken control of your thoughts, you have the power to let them go.

Joanna, a reader of the PurposeFairy blog, knows about

this all too well. When she was eight years old, Joanna was very close to being raped, but luckily for her, her best friend came to her rescue. Even though she was spared, that traumatic experience had a huge impact on Joanna and her life. From that moment on, she started building many walls and barriers between herself and the world around her. She didn't want to be hurt again.

In her twenties, when she gave birth to her baby girl, she knew one thing for sure: she wanted to be a loving mother for her child. But as years went by, she began to realize that her fears were interfering with her ability to love her daughter as much as she deserved to be loved. That's when she slowly started to dismantle the walls she had built to keep the pain away, and began to give love not only to her daughter, but also to herself and everyone around her. It took work, and time, but she is now more available to her child, and more whole within herself.

If you want to be happy, if you want to experience the many wonders of life, and if you want to feel what it really feels like to be fully alive, you have to let go of fear. You have to tear down all the walls you have built between you and the world around you and you have to allow yourself to be vulnerable. You have to allow yourself to be fully seen. You can't serve two masters. You have to choose one—fear or love—and based on the one you choose your life will either be happy or unhappy.

THE PATH TO "GIVING UP"

1. Take a Trip to the End of Your Life

Almost everything—all external expectations, all pride, all fear of embarrassment or failure—these things just fall away in the face of death, leaving only what is truly important. Remembering that you are going to die is the best way I know to avoid the trap of thinking you have something to lose. You are already naked. There is no reason not to follow your heart.

—STEVE JOBS

Close your eyes for a little while and see in your mind's eye the image of you twenty, thirty, fifty or even sixty years from now. You are on your deathbed, ready to depart this world.

Surrounded by the people you love, your friends and family, you begin to remember all the things you did throughout your life, and all the things you were too afraid to do.

Your whole life flashes before your eyes, and all of a sudden you are able to see the big picture.

Seeing all that you see and knowing all that you know, you suddenly realize:

"I could've done it all. I could've achieved it all!"

Detached from all your fears and fully present in the now, for the first time ever you can see things crystal clear.

All your past fears, all your doubts and all your insecurities, they all look so small and insignificant. None of it seems to matter anymore. Your fears no longer frighten you, you no longer feel scared. This realization brings with it a great sense of relief but also an overwhelming feeling of deep sadness:

"Where did my life go?"

"What have I done?"

"I could've been so much happier."

"I could've done it all."

"It's too late for me now."

"I can't go back. I can't undo what was already done . . ."

Your life has an expiration date. You're not going to live forever, none of us are. And when the time comes for you to leave everything behind, when death comes knocking at your door, everything will fall away, leaving only what is truly important. But why wait until it is too late?

Why wait for your whole life to flash before your eyes to finally realize that fear is not worth clinging to? Why wait until it is too late to realize that love is the only thing that's real, the only thing that matters? And that fear is nothing but an illusion.

Let go of it, and surrender it away.

2. Live Your Life Moment to Moment

> You must live in the present, launch yourself on every wave, find your eternity in each moment. Fools stand on their island of opportunities and look toward another land. There is no other land; there is no other life but this.
>
> —HENRY DAVID THOREAU

Each day presents us with a new beginning—the opportunity to create something new, something better. To be born again and to remember who we truly are underneath all our fears, doubts and insecurities. Each day you are given a new opportunity to leave behind all illusions and create a better life for yourself. With each day comes a new chance for you to unlearn all the fearful things that you have learned; to replace your fears with love, and your sorrows with laughter; to let go of everything that no longer serves you and to put your faith in love once more.

Take advantage of this opportunity.

Don't let the troubles of yesterday occupy your mind today. Forget about your past fears, forget about yesterday's worries and make room in your heart for love. Put your past fears aside. Die to the past each night and allow yourself to be born again next morning.

Be led by your hopes, dreams and aspirations, not by your fears, problems and insecurities.

Fill each day with love, joy and laughter, not with fear, regret and resentment.

Be like a newborn baby. Look with eyes of wonder at the world around you. Look at everything and everyone and do your best to perceive the whole world through eyes of love. With no past and with no reasons to fear.

> Fear is not of the present but only of the past and future, which do not exist. There is no fear in the present when each instant stands clear and separated from the past, without its shadow reaching out into the future. Each instant is a clean, untarnished birth... And the present extends forever. It is so beautiful and so clean and free of guilt that nothing but happiness is there. No darkness is remembered, and immortality and joy are now.
>
> —*A COURSE IN MIRACLES*

3. Fear Is Just an Illusion; Love Is the Only Thing That's Real

There are two basic motivating forces: fear and love. When we are afraid, we pull back from life. When we are in love, we open to all that life has to offer with passion, excitement, and acceptance. We need to learn to love ourselves first, in all our glory and our imperfections. If we cannot love ourselves, we cannot fully open to our ability to love others or our potential to create. Evolution and all hopes for a better world rest in the fearlessness and open-hearted vision of people who embrace life.

—JOHN LENNON

No matter how real your fears might seem, and no matter how hard your mind might try to convince you of their authenticity, the truth of the matter is that fear is nothing but a learned behavior. It's nothing but an illusion, an illusion created by your mind. While love is the only thing that's real, the only thing that matters.

Love is present within each and every one of us. We were all born with this emotion. While fear is nothing but a learned behavior, something we attached ourselves to as we started to experience life, observing and interacting with the world around us. And in a controversial experiment called the "Little Albert" experiment, the famous behavioral psychologist John Watson, together with his assistant Rosalie Raynor, proved just that—that fear is a learned behavior.

They exposed this little boy to a series of stimuli including a white rat, a rabbit, a monkey, masks and burning newspapers. At first, the boy showed no fear of those objects. However, the next time he was exposed to the rat, Watson made a loud noise by hitting a metal pipe with a hammer. Hearing the loud noise, Albert got scared and began to cry. After Watson repeatedly paired the white rat with the loud noise, the boy began to cry every time he saw the rat. After conditioning, the little boy feared not just the white rat, but a wide variety of similar white, furry objects, such as a rabbit, a dog, and even a ball of cotton.

Underneath all your fears, doubts and insecurities there's nothing but pure and unconditional love. Love for yourself, love for those around you and love for life itself. But because you have been clinging to fear for so long, you can no longer remember this truth. You can no longer make the distinction between what is real and what is not.

Just as John Lennon once stated, there are two basic motivating forces, two emotions we can express, and these two emotions are FEAR and LOVE. All the other emotions with which we are all so familiar are nothing more than subcategories of these two. Where there is LOVE, we may have peace, joy, contentment, serenity and forgiveness, while on the other hand, where there is fear, we will have anxiety, sadness, depression, fatigue, judgment and guilt.

Where there is LOVE, fear cannot survive, and where there is fear, LOVE cannot exist.

You are not your fears; you are not your past; and you are not your doubts, insecurities, excuses and limitations. You are beauty and perfection. You are made of love and made to love.

You are love!

Let go of fear and allow love to rule your world. Let go of fear and allow love to show you the way back onto your life path.

4. Let Love Tear Down
All the Walls You Have Built

> The walls we build around us to keep sadness out also keep out the joy.
>
> —JIM ROHN

Open the door to your heart and let it stay wide open. Tear down all those fearful walls you have built between you and the world around you.

Build fewer walls and more bridges.

Don't hide yourself from yourself. Don't hide yourself from life. Don't hide yourself from love. Allow your own light to shine as brightly as possible. Allow yourself to be fully seen. Allow yourself to be vulnerable. Tear down all the walls you have built to numb yourself in order to keep suffering away from you, and allow love back into your life. Allow love to show you how it feels to be fully alive.

Let the world see into your naked soul and beautiful heart. Let yourself experience life fully. Understand that love is life and life is love. And if you give up on love, you give up on life.

Infuse love into your life. Pour love into everything you do and everything you are. Pour love into yourself, into your relationships, your work, your environment and into your life. Pour love onto your past, your wounds, your struggles and your fears. Infuse love into every experience and every interaction, either good or bad, and let all your fears be healed by love.

Offer your love to everyone you come in contact with, not necessarily because they are worthy of your love, but because love is all that you have to offer. Because love is all that you have to give.

Take your focus away from all the things that scare you, away from all the fearful stories your mind has been fabricating for all these years, and start focusing on the things you love instead. Speak only of that which brings you joy, peace and happiness. Do work that has meaning, work that feeds your soul. Surround yourself with beauty.

Let go of fear and allow love to govern all areas of your life. Love all your fears away. Love until your heart breaks and then love some more. Love until there's nothing left in you but love.

Give up the fear within and allow the real you to awaken. Allow the real you to be, to love, to play, to create and to live the life it came here to create.

Don't be afraid of love, for love can never hurt you. Love can only love.

Chapter 3

GIVE UP YOUR LIMITING BELIEFS

> It's not the events of our lives that shape us, but our
> beliefs as to what those events mean.
>
> —TONY ROBBINS

MY STORY

Even though I have always feared my father, and even though whenever he was at home I would try my best to run and hide away from him, deep down inside I had always hoped that one day he was going to change. I had always hoped that maybe one day he was going to come home and start treating me and my family with the love, kindness and compassion we all deserved. But he never did.

My father died before any of these things could happen. He died and left me thinking that there was something seriously wrong with me and that the reason why he couldn't love me wasn't because he was incapable of love, but because of this something that was wrong with me. He couldn't love me because I wasn't a lovable person.

And I carried this dreadful and toxic belief with me for years and years, thinking that I was to blame for everything that had happened in the past and thinking that if my own father couldn't love me, nobody ever would.

I physically almost couldn't open my mouth to talk to anyone about all the pain and sadness that I had been accumulating in my heart for a long time. I didn't have the courage to share my thoughts, struggles and inner turmoil with anyone. And so I carried the heavy burden with me, believing that I was all alone and that nobody was ever going to love me, that nobody was ever going to understand me or care about me.

. . .

Years of conditioning made me acquire very limiting beliefs, and one of them was that I was not worthy of being cared for. This belief was so firmly part of my mindset that one day I was surprised by an incident in school.

"What's happening to you?" I heard my History teacher say to me one day, when I was mentally checked out. I snapped back to reality, looked around me and saw the eyes of classmates gazing back at me as I sat at my desk.

"Your grades are very low.

Do you realize that if you continue like this you risk failing the class?

You risk repeating the entire year!

If you don't study you're going to have to repeat fifth grade.

Is that what you want?"

It took me a while to reply . . . I was too confused by the fact that she was showing any interest at all in me and my school situation. She cared, and it stunned me, because up until that point I had believed nobody cared.

"No. I don't want that," I said to her even though I didn't really mean it.

"I don't want to repeat the year."

LESSONS IN LETTING GO

The moment you doubt whether you can fly, you cease forever to be able to do it.

—J. M. BARRIE, *PETER PAN*

Living in an environment where there always seemed to be an abundance of painful and traumatic experiences but a lack of happy and loving ones, I developed from a very young age all kinds of limiting beliefs about life being hard, about me not being good enough, smart enough, worthy enough or beautiful enough.

When my father died, thinking that I was all alone and feeling overwhelmed by everything that had happened to me up until that moment, I didn't really seem to care about anything or anyone anymore. Probably because I believed that nobody cared about me either. But I was wrong.

I had to go through many challenges, and I had to inflict

a lot of pain on those around me and myself, before I finally understood that people were treating me the way I was expecting to be treated, that life was giving me that which I was feeling worthy of receiving. So I had to learn to cleanse my mind. I had to change the way I was thinking and I had to let go of many of my old and toxic beliefs so that I could make room in my life for new, healthy, positive and empowering beliefs.

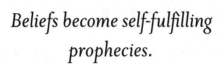

Beliefs become self-fulfilling prophecies.

Beliefs become self-fulfilling prophecies. They shape our reality, they make us who we are. And if we really want to create a better life for ourselves and for those we love, we have to make sure that the beliefs we hold on to are serving us well and that they aren't sabotaging our happiness, health and well-being.

. . .

We create our lives with our thoughts. We shape our lives based on the beliefs we have. And if our beliefs are limiting and negative, so will our lives be. Life doesn't discriminate. Life gives you the things, people and experiences you feel worthy and deserving of receiving. Life treats you the way you expect to be treated, the way you believe you deserve to be treated. And as long as you perceive and believe that you are unworthy and undeserving of the many wonderful and precious gifts life has to offer you, life will prove you right.

Rosanna, a young woman who wrote to me recently, told me how she was always "reminded" by her mother of the fact that all men are cheaters and liars and that no matter how honest, transparent, loving and respectful you are toward them, they will still lie to you. With this limiting belief deeply engraved in her mind, Rosanna unknowingly started attracting in her life exactly this type of man. She went from relationship to relationship, each one ending for the same reason: she was cheated on.

After a while, she began to question whether the men's behavior had anything to do with her own personal beliefs and expectations. With this question constantly weighing on her, she decided to play a trick on her mind.

Whenever she would catch herself thinking that all men are cheaters and liars, she would immediately shift her focus to new thoughts: "Men are loyal, trustworthy, loving and respectful." She kept repeating this to herself day after day and month after month, and eventually she began to see proof of this new belief all around her. And that is how she met her husband—a wonderful, loyal and loving man who is not only treating her as if she's the most beautiful and wonderful woman in the world, but also reinforcing the belief that men can be trusted, and that she truly has the power to change her mind and her life.

。　。　。

It can be so easy to fall into the trap of believing that you and your past are one and that if you were treated unfairly then you will be treated unfairly now and in the future.

It can be so easy to believe that your self-worth comes from your net worth and that happiness comes from having big, shiny and expensive things, lots of them.

It can be so easy to fall into the trap of believing that who you are is not good enough, smart enough or deserving enough.

It can be so easy to believe that if you have rich parents it can only mean that you are smart and worthy of respect, love and admiration, and that everyone around you is going to love and approve of you.

It can be so easy to believe that being vulnerable, talking about your thoughts and feelings and allowing yourself to be fully seen by those around you, is an act of weakness, something to be ashamed about.

It can be so easy to let others define you, to raise and lower yourself to the level of their expectations.

But even though all of these things might be easy to do, it doesn't mean that we should continue to do them.

The beliefs of the past don't have to be the same as the beliefs of the present. And they surely don't have to be the same beliefs we will have in the future.

Change the quality of your beliefs and the quality of your life will change too.

THE PATH TO "GIVING UP"

1. Thoughts Have Creative Power

Watch your thoughts for they become words. Watch your words for they become actions. Watch your actions for they become habits. Watch your habits for they become your character. And watch your character for it becomes your destiny. What we think, we become. My father always said that . . . and I think I am fine.

—MARGARET THATCHER

Your thoughts have the power to lift you up or tear you down; to boost your self-esteem and improve your self-image and confidence, or lower your confidence, damage your self-image and ruin your whole life. That's how powerful your thoughts are. And if you want to improve the quality of your life, if you want to let go of your many limiting beliefs and create healthier, more positive and empowering ones, all you have to do is improve the quality of the thoughts you think and the words you speak.

If there are limits in your mind, there will be limits in your life; if there is poverty thinking in your mind, there will be poverty in your life; if there is fear in your mind, fear will also be present in your life. For something to exist in the material world, it has to exist in consciousness first.

The life you are now living is a result of your thinking. Everything was created with your thoughts. And just as everything was created with your thoughts, everything can also be changed by your thoughts.

If you don't like something about yourself, about your life, or if you think there are things that you can't do because you were told that they were impossible for you to achieve, all you have to do is correct the thoughts you think and the words you speak. By doing so, you will create new and healthier beliefs, beliefs that will later on give you the strength, courage and confidence to start doing the things you once thought impossible. Beliefs that will make you realize that Muhammad Ali was right: "Impossible is just a big word thrown around by small men who find it easier to live in the world they've been given than to explore the power they have to change it. Impossible is not a fact. It's an opinion. Impossible is not a declaration. It's a dare. Impossible is potential. Impossible is temporary. Impossible is nothing."

Impossible is nothing. What you think of yourself is everything. Change your thoughts and you change your beliefs. Change your beliefs and you change your whole life.

2. Choose One Thought Over Another

A belief is only a thought that you keep thinking. So as you keep thinking this thought, you keep vibrationally attracting relative to that thought. So you confirm your own beliefs again and again and again and again and again. That's why someone who believes in cancer can

confirm that belief, or someone who believes in rob-
bery can confirm that belief. So everything is a sort of
confirmation of belief.

—ESTHER HICKS

Don't let your mind trick you into thinking that just because
you couldn't do something in the past, you will never be able
to do that something in the present or in the future. Always remember that there are no limits to who you can be, to what you
can do and to the life you can live, except those limits you
yourself impose on yourself.

No matter how deeply engraved in your mind your limiting beliefs may be, and no matter how long you have been
holding on to them, becoming aware of the fact that your many
limiting beliefs were once only thoughts that you kept thinking can make this whole process of letting go a lot easier.

Life is a lot like a game. Once you learn the rules of the
game, life seems to get a lot easier and you start to have a lot of
fun. And the most important rule of the game is to pay close attention to the thoughts that run through your mind and to make
sure that you feed your mind with healthy, empowering and
positive thoughts. Healthy thoughts, healthy mind, healthy life.

Just as you've learned to cling to all kinds of limiting beliefs about why you can't do, be and have many of the things
you say you want to do, be and have, in the same way you can
learn to let go of those beliefs and create healthier, more positive ones, beliefs that will help you craft your life in a way you
never thought was possible.

By changing the thoughts that run through your mind, one by one choosing positive thoughts over negative ones, in time you will end up giving up your old and limiting beliefs.

All you have to do is pay close attention to your thoughts and slowly replace the negative ones with positive ones. Replace "I can't" with "I can," "impossible" with "I'm possible," "I'm unworthy" with "I'm worthy," and so on.

Start small. Change one thought at a time, one limiting belief at a time. And as you get better and better at doing this, you will see how many of the things you once thought were impossible will soon enough become possible. And how many of the things, people and experiences you once saw as being out of reach will very soon start manifesting in your life.

As a single footstep will not make a path on the earth, so a single thought will not make a pathway in the mind. To make a deep physical path, we walk again and again. To make a deep mental path, we must think over and over the kind of thoughts we wish to dominate our lives.

—HENRY DAVID THOREAU

3. There's a Genius in All of Us

All children are born geniuses; 9,999 out of every 10,000 are swiftly, inadvertently degeniusized by grownups.

—BUCKMINSTER FULLER

Years ago, an incredible study was made at Harvard University, called Project Zero, in which Howard Gardner, together with his colleagues, found that every child is born a genius, across multiple intelligences, but that by the age of twenty, the percentage of geniuses within a population has been whittled down to 10 percent . . . and over the age of twenty, only 2 percent retain their genius ability.

What this study did was prove that intelligence is not an inherited trait, nor is it something that only special people possess, but rather there is genius in each and every one of us.

This is something you should never doubt. Something you should never forget. And even though at times your mind will try to convince you that there's nothing unique and special about you, you should never doubt that there truly is. You should never doubt that there is something in you that is unique, powerful and of great value, that there is a beautiful reason for your existence and a great purpose for your life, because there is.

We are all born gifted; we are all born geniuses. There is something unique, valuable and very precious in each and every one of us. We all possess unique gifts and talents that are meant to be our gifts to the world. And by putting our fears, excuses and limitations behind us, by making a commitment to ourselves to do the necessary work toward remembering who we truly are and toward re-becoming the wonderful and precious beings we were born to be, we will be able to tap into these inner gifts and talents, reigniting our inner fire, rekindling our inner flame and claiming back our genius and our personal power. And in time we will be able to realize that who we are matters, and that the work we hold in our hearts is of great value and of great importance.

4. Who You Are Matters

> If a man is called to be a street sweeper, he should sweep streets even as Michelangelo painted, or Beethoven composed music or Shakespeare wrote poetry. He should sweep streets so well that all the hosts of heaven and earth will pause to say, "Here lived a great street sweeper who did his job well."
> —MARTIN LUTHER KING JR.

There's no such thing as intelligent and less intelligent people. There's no such thing as worthy and unworthy people. There's no such thing as valuable and less valuable people. There's no such thing as people who can make the impossible possible and people who can't. There's no such thing as special and less special people. These are nothing but mind-created barriers and limitations—limitations that are meant to keep us stuck in a very dark, lonely and unhappy place.

There's something unique and precious about each and every one of us. We are all valuable human beings; we are all intelligent and capable of achieving many beautiful and wonderful things. We each have a very important role to play in this world, and who we are matters.

Who you are matters. What you know matters. Your unique gifts and talents matter. Your presence and your work matter, and whether you believe it or not, the world needs you.

We all have our own piece to contribute to this big puzzle called life. And if we choose to cling to all kinds of fears, excuses and limitations, if we continue to settle for way less than we are worth, living a mediocre life and always thinking that who we are is not enough, then this puzzle will never be complete. And we will never know what true happiness is really all about.

The world needs you to be you.

The world needs you to be you, to do your part and to play your role as beautifully as possible. So put all your limitations aside. Cleanse your inner vision and start thinking in terms of "I'm possible" instead of "impossible." Start thinking in terms of "I'm worthy" instead of "I'm unworthy." Stop settling for way less than you are worth and allow the real you to shine. Unleash your inner power, your inner beauty and genius, and allow the world to see the real you.

Cleanse yourself. Remove all the layers of mud that have been covering you for all this time—this mud representing all the limitations, all the bad programming and all the negative past conditioning, and start living life from a place of love, truth, authenticity and inner power, no longer from a place of fear and limitation.

5. Imagine Your Way to a Better Life

You possess what the rest of Nature does not possess—Imagination—the instrument by which you create your world. Your imagination is the instrument, the means, whereby your redemption from slavery, sickness, and poverty is effected. If you refuse to assume the responsibility of the incarnation of a new and higher concept of yourself, then you reject the means, the only means, whereby your redemption—that is, the attainment of your ideal—can be effected.

—NEVILLE GODDARD

Ask yourself:

"If there were no limits to what I can do, be and have, how would my life look?"

How would your life look if there were no limits to who you could be, to what you could create? How would it feel to have the life you say you want to live?

Play this game for a little while.

Forget about what is. Forget about your dreadful and cruel reality, your fears, worries and problems, and allow yourself to do this mental exercise for a little while. Allow yourself to feel in your body all the feelings that would come from having transcended your limitations and from having your dreams come true. Feel within you the feelings that would come from having all those wonderful things happen to you and allow those feelings to become part of who you are.

See in your mind's eye the life you would love to live, the person you want to become and the relationships you want to have. See yourself being surrounded by beauty, love, wealth and abundance, and allow yourself to be in that space, to know what it would be like to live a life without limits.

Albert Einstein once said that "imagination is more important than knowledge. For knowledge is limited to all we now know and understand, while imagination embraces the entire world, and all there ever will be to know and understand." And the truth of the matter is that imagination is your most precious and valuable gift, the instrument by which you create your world. And the more you learn to use this valuable gift, the better your life will get and the happier you will become.

Let your imagination run wild. Don't censor yourself. Don't place any limits on yourself and on what you want to be, do and have. And know that, as William Arthur Ward said, "if you can imagine it, you can achieve it. If you can dream it, you can become it."

Understand that you weren't born to suffer, and you surely weren't born to live an unhappy and meaningless life. You were born to thrive, to let your own light shine and to become the best you can be.

You were born to thrive.

· · ·

Live your life in a sublime spirit of confidence and de-
termination; disregard appearances, conditions, in fact
all evidence of your senses that deny the fulfillment of
your desire. Rest in the assumption that you are already what you want to be, for in that determined assumption you and your Infinite Being are merged in
creative unity, and with your Infinite Being all things
are possible.

—NEVILLE GODDARD

Claim yourself to be the thing desired. Change your perception of yourself, your state of consciousness, and claim
yourself to be that which you want to be, do and have. Because
by doing so you will start to attract into your life the right
thoughts, people and circumstances, and eventually all the
things that you once saw in your mind's eye will be material-
izing in the external world.

If you want things to be moving in a new direction, if you
want to make some changes for the better in your life, if you
want to see your world change, you need to work on becoming
that which you want to experience in the physical world.

Give up your limitations. Put aside all your thoughts about
how you are supposedly flawed, unworthy or undeserving of
anything good, and soon enough you'll discover that you too
have something very special and very valuable to offer to those
around you and to yourself. You too are special.

Chapter 4

GIVE UP YOUR EXCUSES

Hold yourself responsible for a higher standard than
anyone else expects of you. Never excuse yourself.

—HENRY WARD BEECHER

MY STORY

I don't know if I ever saw myself as someone who came up
with excuses. The way I saw it, life treated me unkindly, and if
I was living a very unhappy life it wasn't because of me. It
wasn't because I was making up excuses, but because that's
how my life was. I was just being "realistic."

Everything seemed to be out of my control. In fact, for a
very long time I lived under the impression that life was happening to me and that I had no say in it whatsoever. I was just
a puppet.

When you get your sense of identity from your past hurts,
your wounds and your struggles, it can be quite impossible to

acknowledge the fact that maybe you are using what happened in the past as an excuse for why you are not living a happier and more meaningful life in the present.

Even though after that whole incident in fifth grade with my History teacher I started to care about my grades and about my school situation, and even though by the time I finished high school I was one of the top students in my class, for some strange reason I still didn't fully believe in myself. I still didn't think I had what it takes to go to a good university.

I remember being in my last year of high school and feeling so scared and so disoriented. Looking at my classmates and seeing how they were all preparing themselves for university, studying very hard and doing their best to make their dreams come true, I realized that I had no dreams and that I wasn't really passionate about anything. I had no idea where I wanted to go to university or whether I was even going to go to one. All kinds of crazy thoughts were running through my mind:

It would be nice to continue to study Architecture . . . but what if I won't be able to handle it? What if it's going to be too hard for me?

The subjects you study while in university are a lot more difficult than the ones you study in high school. And I'm sure I'm going to fail many classes.

No, I really don't think this is going to work out. I really don't think I have what it takes to go to university.

Plus, my mom can't really afford to put me through school in another city, so I should just stay home . . .

If all throughout secondary school and high school I felt safe and quite comfortable with where I was and with how my life was unfolding, once I finished high school, I went back to feeling scared, alone, lost and disconnected. I went back to being that same insecure little girl that I was when my father was alive.

. . .

Thinking that things weren't going to work out for me if I decided to continue to study Architecture and that my mom couldn't really afford to pay for my studies and for all the expenses that would come from me living in a different city, I decided to take the easy out. I decided to go to university in my hometown and study History, which I dropped out of after just a few months without telling anyone.

I stayed home for two years after that, feeling like a total failure, damaging my self-esteem and confidence, falling into the trap of thinking that my life was ruined. Instead of using the same mentality I had used in fifth grade when I was so close to failing History class, and instead of looking for ways to make the "impossible" possible, I decided to give up on myself once again, allowing my fears, doubts, limitations and excuses to hold me back in life and forcing myself to walk on a path that wasn't mine to walk on.

By using one excuse after another and by believing every limiting thought that was running through my mind, I ended up making many bad choices.

After two years of staying home and doing absolutely nothing with my life, influenced by the "good" opinions of those around me, I decided to go to university once again. This time to study Economics, something I was later going to regret.

LESSONS IN LETTING GO

People spend too much time finding other people to blame, too much energy finding excuses for not being what they are capable of being, and not enough energy putting themselves on the line, growing out of the past, and getting on with their lives.

—J. MICHAEL STRACZYNSKI

A lot of times we limit ourselves because of the many excuses we use. Instead of growing and working on improving ourselves and our lives, we get stuck, lying to ourselves, using all kinds of excuses—excuses that 99.9 percent of the time are not even real.

We fall into the trap of thinking that we don't have enough time to do the things we want to do, that we're not ready to take the necessary steps that will contribute to our growth and happiness, that nobody will help and support us, that we don't have the necessary resources, knowledge, time and so on. And because of our attachment to all of these excuses and limitations we sell ourselves short, settling for way less than we are worth and living a life that is not ours to live.

* * *

When you've lived most of your life in an environment where excuses were part of your everyday existence and where most people perceived themselves as victims of their circumstances, it can be quite challenging not to perceive your excuses, fears and limitations as truths. But you have to be willing to let go of your excuses if you want to create something new, something fresh and something better.

I wasted so many years of my life because of the many excuses I was so deeply attached to. I did things that had no real value to me and lived a life that had no purpose and no meaning.

Thinking that I didn't have what it takes to continue to study Architecture, that I could never afford to move to a different city, and that I wasn't really capable of living all alone among strangers, I gave up. I gave up on life and myself without even questioning my thoughts, beliefs and excuses, thinking that that was the right thing to do, that I wasn't worthy and deserving of a better life and that I shouldn't even dare to dream of one. And I did that for more than twenty-five years. Using my past as an excuse for why my present wasn't better and why I wasn't living a happy, meaningful and balanced life.

Frank, a man in his forties who reached out to me, had a similar struggle.

Having been raised in a rough neighborhood, and constantly exposed to physical, verbal and emotional abuse from his parents, Frank used his past as an excuse to drop out of school and start making a living by selling drugs. That's what he did for more than fifteen years, even though he was aware that it wasn't the right thing to do. His excuse was always the same: "I don't know how to do anything else. I don't have any skills for making a decent living."

His life took a different turn when he was involved in a shooting and was severely wounded in the chest. When he was rushed to the hospital, the doctors did everything to save him, and when he was finally stable, he was told that his being alive was a miracle and that he should be grateful for being given a second chance at life. After almost losing his life, Frank decided he needed to stop making excuses, give it all up and make a fresh start. He moved to a different town, went back to school and finished college as one of the top students in the class. He now runs his own business and is living a much happier and more fulfilled life than he could have ever imagined.

There *is* always a way out. No matter how old or young you might be, no matter how many mistakes you might have made in the past, no matter if you think that you don't have what it takes to change your life for the better, no matter if you think people won't support you, if you really want to make something happen, you will put all your excuses behind you and you will find a way to make the impossible possible.

Where there is a will, there is always a way, and once you start giving up your excuses, you will be able to see things clearly. You will find The Way.

THE PATH TO "GIVING UP"

1. All Excuses Are Misalignment

All excuses are misalignment. Words like "difficult," "risky," "can't," "too weak," "too dumb" and "too complicated" do not apply to the divine mind. I urge you to reharmonize with energy that can do anything and everything, for this is your original nature.

—WAYNE DYER

Who you are underneath it all knows no limits, no fear and no limitations. And whenever you choose to use all kinds of excuses for why you can't be, do or have something, you are in fact moving away from your true power, disconnecting from your true self and building a false identity for yourself. An identity that will only weaken you, causing you to see yourself as being small, powerless and insignificant. Your excuses keep you from being true to yourself, from listening to the messages of your heart and soul, and they keep you from remembering that within you lies both the power and the ability to create the beautiful and loving life you deep down know that you deserve to live. And that is why it so important to learn to differentiate between your true self and your mentally constructed self, between what is real and what is not, between what is fear and what is love, between what is truth and what is illusion.

Know that you have your unique path to walk upon, your own purpose to fulfill, and that whenever you attach yourself to your excuses, to your many fears and limitations, you move away from your true nature and away from your life path. You stop being in harmony with who you are, and you start living a life that is not yours to live. And that's how life starts to become a struggle.

All the discomfort, unease, pain and unhappiness you experience whenever you cling to your many excuses is caused by your efforts to build a false identity and a fearful life for yourself, a life that has no purpose and no meaning, a life that is built on fear and doubt instead of love and trust.

Dare to listen to what your heart has to say. Reharmonize with energy that can do anything and everything and give yourself permission to love, to grow, to evolve and to live your life to the fullest.

Get into the habit of questioning every thought you think and every belief you have, especially those thoughts and beliefs that hold you back in life. Learn to reflect on the things your mind tells you. Learn to assess yourself, your thoughts, your beliefs and your excuses.

Let go of the need to use words like "It's too difficult," "It won't happen to me," "I don't have the time," "I don't have the energy," "Nobody will help me," "I'm too old," and so on, and allow your courageous heart and loving soul to lead the way.

When we know who we are, we can overcome our
fears and insecurities. We surpass our smaller selves . . .
The answers to the questions of what to say, what to

do, whom to let in, and whom to keep out become a clear and simple matter of listening to our hearts. That inner voice helps us align with our purpose . . . The voice is there. We just need to listen to it. When we do that, we live in fearlessness.

—ARIANNA HUFFINGTON

2. Assess Yourself

It is necessary . . . for a man to go away by himself . . . to sit on a rock . . . and ask, "Who am I, where have I been, and where am I going?"

—CARL SANDBURG

In his book *Excuses Begone*, Wayne Dyer suggests that we should always question our excuses by asking ourselves these two simple yet powerful questions:

"Is it true?"

"Can I be 100 percent sure it is true?"

Grab a pen and a piece of paper and write down all the reasons why you think you are not living the life you deep down inside want to live.

Here are a few examples of excuses:

> ➤ What if things don't go as planned?
> ➤ What will people think of me?
> ➤ I can't afford it.
> ➤ I don't have the time.

➤ I am too busy. Too old. Too tired.

➤ It can never happen to me.

➤ It never happened before.

➤ My family won't support me.

➤ I can't do it because of my past.

➤ I'm not ready.

➤ I don't have what it takes.

Be open, transparent and fully honest with yourself. Confront, list and question all your excuses. And once you're done, look over your list and ask yourself:

"Is it true?"

"Can I be 100 percent sure it is true?"

Are you sure that the things you think about yourself, the things you think you can't do, be or have are true? Can you be 100 percent sure that they are true?

3. Replace Your Excuses with Positive Affirmations

You will be a failure, until you impress the subconscious with the conviction you are a success. This is done by making an affirmation which "clicks."

—FLORENCE SCOVEL SHINN

Don't make excuses for why you can't get something done. Focus on all the reasons why you must make it happen, and in the end you will find a way. If you know the *why* you can handle any *how*.

If you know the why you can handle any how.

Start by taking a good look at your list of reasons why something can't be done. See how you can replace those excuses with positive and empowering affirmations, affirmations that will inspire you to give up all your excuses and start focusing on many of the reasons why it *can* be done.

Here are some examples:

I don't have the time ➤ I have all the time in the world to do all the things I want to do and more.

I am afraid ➤ Fear is just an illusion. Love is the only thing that's real. If I focus on love, I will be safe.

My family won't support me ➤ My family wants me to be happy, and I know they will support me in my search for happiness.

I am too old ➤ Age is just a number. An issue of mind over matter, as Mark Twain said, and if I don't mind, it doesn't matter.

Make the unconscious conscious. See your excuses for what they are—excuses. Take control over your own thoughts and over your own mind.

Replace your many excuses with positive affirmations and then choose to act upon these positive affirmations. Act upon your heart's desire. Do the things you need to do in order to get where you want to get. Read the books you need to read, contact the people you need to contact, build the skills you need to build. Find the right people. Ask the right questions. Do whatever it takes to move yourself closer to living the life you deserve to live. And trust that with every step you take, your excuses will disappear, your life situation will improve, and you will move closer and closer to the life you want to live.

4. Take the First Step in Faith

Take the first step in faith. You don't have to see the whole staircase, just take the first step.
—MARTIN LUTHER KING JR.

Take at least one step each day to move yourself further and further away from your excuses and closer to creating and living a meaningful and happy life.

If there is something you want to do, be or have, and if you feel it in your heart that you and those around you will benefit from your being, doing or having this thing, act on it. Work on making this thing become reality.

Don't spend too much time thinking about how it will happen and about the many reasons why it can't happen to you. Instead, focus mainly on the end result. Don't worry about the

HOW. Learn to delegate authority to life itself. Focus on WHAT you want and WHY you want what you want. And know that if your intentions are aligned with who you truly are, and if having your dreams come true will benefit you and those around you, life will lead you in the right direction, taking good care of you and providing you the right tools, the right people and the necessary experiences that will help you reach your destination. So find the courage to take risks, to get out of your comfort zone and to do the things your heart is asking you to do.

> Take the first step, and your mind will mobilize all its forces to your aid. But the first essential is that you begin. Once the battle is started, all that is within and without you will come to your assistance.
>
> —ROBERT COLLIER

Follow your inner guidance; trust your intuition. Seek to believe only those thoughts that come from a place of love, power and encouragement. Seek to only act on those thoughts that come from your loving soul and authentic self.

Align your mind with your heart and your body with your soul. Align yourself with who you truly are, and know that by doing so, you will immediately become conscious of the abundant life within you, and all of a sudden all kinds of wonderful things will start happening to you because of you. The right people will start to show up in your life, the right books will "fall" into your hands, the perfect circumstances will be offered to you . . . and before you know it, many of the things you once thought were impossible for you to be, do and have will manifest themselves into your life.

So take the first step in faith. You don't have to see the whole staircase, just take the first step. And in time you will realize that your faith will guide you in the right direction, and as a result of that, life will start showering you with all kinds of wonderful and magical gifts. Gifts that will make your life and the life of those you love so much brighter and happier.

Chapter 5

GIVE UP YOUR RESISTANCE TO CHANGE

We delight in the beauty of the butterfly, but rarely admit the changes it has gone through to achieve that beauty.

—MAYA ANGELOU

MY STORY

I wasn't really interested in boys while growing up. Having had a father who showed no love and affection toward me, and having been abused all throughout my childhood years, I developed this belief that all men were cruel and heartless and that I needed to stay as far away from them as possible. And so I made sure not to get close to any boy and not to let any boy come near me. I was strongly resistant to change in this regard, and afraid of being loved or falling in love, thinking that love equaled pain and that if I made the mistake of falling in love with anyone, I would eventually end up just like my mother. And I didn't want that.

But love is a lot stronger than fear. Love is who we all are and love is what we all seek, and even though I tried very hard to stay away from it, in the fall of 2003, the same year I finished high school and the same year I decided to drop out of university, love was going to smoothly "force" itself on me. Making me realize that there wasn't a more beautiful and precious feeling than that of loving and being loved.

. . .

It was a chilly evening when Stefan and I first met. I remember seeing him waiting for me in front of this building very close to my place and thinking to myself:

Oh boy. This guy is so not my type.

Why in the world did I agree to this date?

Change seemed on the horizon, and I tried to resist.

But like many times before, I assumed incorrectly.

Even though at first sight he didn't really look like someone I would be interested in, once our date was over and once I got home, I realized that I actually liked him.

I don't know if it was his sense of humor, his beautiful mind, his way of thinking and looking at things or his innocent smile and beautiful big green eyes, but what I do know is that I felt that there was something special about him, something different.

He was very charming, affectionate, kind and compassionate— qualities that I wasn't really accustomed to—and even though

I didn't expect it to happen, after three or four months of dating, I fell head over heels in love with him.

We spent almost three years in that beautiful emotional space. Getting drunk with love, making each other so happy and feeling as if the whole world was ours. Those were probably some of the most beautiful years of my life, the best days of my life. And even though I desperately hoped that things would never change between us and that we were going to stay in love forever, life had different things in store for us.

In the winter of 2005, Stefan decided to go work in the U.S. for six months, leaving me behind and making me feel as if I had lost a very precious part of me. The moment he gave me the news I felt devastated.

We spoke quite often while he was gone, and thankfully, in the summer of 2006 he came home. Not to stay, but to take me with him back to the U.S. to live there together.

•   •   •

For a very long time I perceived change as something painful and traumatic. Having been exposed to so many shocking and upsetting experiences all throughout my childhood years and having felt so much pain and so much suffering whenever things did change in my life, our home and our family, I began to associate change with pain and suffering. Not wanting to suffer again, and not wanting to be exposed to more pain and trauma, I tried very hard to resist going to the U.S. with my boyfriend.

I felt paralyzed by fear. In those moments fear became a lot bigger and a lot more powerful than the love I had in my heart for him.

"I can't go," I kept telling myself daily. And:

"I have to stay."

"This is where I belong."

"My home is here."

"If I stay here, I will be safe."

Believing that if things remained the same, and if I continued to live my life in the same environment and in the same way, I was going to be safe and protected from life's many challenges, I resisted signing the contract for the job that awaited me, hoping that by doing so I was going to be forever safe.

LESSONS IN LETTING GO

The person who risks nothing, does nothing, has nothing, is nothing, and becomes nothing. He may avoid suffering and sorrow, but he simply cannot learn and feel and change and grow and love and live.

—LEO F. BUSCAGLIA

It took my boyfriend almost two months to convince me that there was nothing to fear and that change was going to bring us both many great things. And even though I eventually signed the job contract and went to the U.S. with him, I had to face many more struggles and even more resistance before I finally realized the futility of resisting and rejecting change.

We are creatures of habit. Most of us live our lives on autopilot, allowing our old programming, our past fears, excuses and limitations, to run, craft and shape our lives. And because we desperately try to keep things from changing and because we desperately try to keep life from taking its natural course, we inflict a lot of unnecessary pain on ourselves and on those we love.

.   .   .

The greater danger for most of us lies not in setting our aim too high and falling short; but in setting our aim too low, and achieving our mark.

—MICHELANGELO

I hear from people from all walks of life who are holding on to something they've outgrown—a job, a partner, a relationship with a parent, a memory. They are in pain, but not for the reason they often think. While the pain can feel like it's coming from the longing for that lost person or emotion, what we're usually experiencing is the agony of holding on to an impossibility. We are working too hard—and causing ourselves to be miserable. The relief we so dearly need will come not from clinging more tightly, but from letting go.

Life is meant to be fully experienced, with good and bad, with both ups and downs, and the more you try to keep life from happening by resisting and fighting change, the more you will continue to suffer and the unhappier your life will get.

Change is a natural process. You can't run away from it, just as you can't run away from life. And if you try, you'll miss out on life and you'll miss out on the great opportunity to know yourself, to be yourself and to love yourself.

THE PATH TO "GIVING UP"

1. Be Honest with Yourself

All changes, even the most longed for, have their melancholy; for what we leave behind us is a part of ourselves; we must die to one life before we can enter another.

—ANATOLE FRANCE

Don't let your biggest fears get in the way of your biggest dreams. Learn to be honest with yourself. Seek to understand what your feelings regarding change are and why you feel the need to run away from change instead of embracing it.

Ask yourself questions like:

➤ What are my thoughts about change?
➤ What is it about change that I find so distasteful and so unappealing?
➤ What do I think will happen if I let go of my resistance to change?
➤ Am I afraid that if I do change I risk losing my

sense of identity and that maybe I won't like the person I become?

➤ Am I afraid that if I step into the unknown and if I start doing things differently I might fail and I won't be able to live with all that guilt and shame?

➤ Do I fear getting hurt and being laughed at?

➤ Am I afraid that if I give up my resistance and invite change into my life I might have to leave behind things, places and people I love?

➤ What am I so afraid of?

Discover what the reasons are behind your resistance and it will become a lot easier to begin to see change not as your enemy but as your friend.

2. Change Is Inevitable— Resisting Change Is a Losing Game

Without accepting the fact that everything changes, we cannot find perfect composure. But unfortunately, although it is true, it is difficult for us to accept it. Because we cannot accept the truth of transience, we suffer.

—SHUNRYU SUZUKI

Whenever life wants you to move in a different direction, whenever you are "asked" to leave your comfort zone and step into the unknown, contrary to what your fears will try to make you believe, you are not being punished. On the contrary, you are given the opportunity to know yourself and to be yourself. You are being given the chance to step back on your life path and align with who you truly are. But if you continue to ignore life's many callings and if you continue to resist change, there will be no remembering. There will be no positive and inspiring transformation taking place within you. There will be no positive change taking place, and your present and future life will continue to be a poor copy of your past.

There's a natural flow to life, and change is meant to help you go with that flow. Get out of your comfort zone and dare to step into the unknown. Dare to do the things that you are afraid of doing.

Don't ignore this opportunity. Don't ignore the chance to remember who you truly are, to bring purpose and meaning back into your life and to live the life you are meant to live. Allow change to take you back home, back where you belong.

Make peace with this idea that everything in life changes. And instead of feeling bitter and resentful toward life and toward change, choose to feel grateful and appreciative toward every experience life sends your way.

3. Assume the Best

> Because your own strength is unequal to the task, do not assume that it is beyond the powers of man; but if anything is within the powers and province of man, believe that it is within your own compass also.
>
> —MARCUS AURELIUS

Instead of creating negative and fearful scenarios about how your whole life will fall apart once you let go of your resistance, and instead of imagining how you will make a fool of yourself once you get out of your comfort zone and step into the unknown, assume the best instead. Expect all kinds of wonderful things to always happen to you. Choose to create positive and empowering scenarios in your mind and play these movies in your head as often as possible.

With every day, work on cleansing your mind of the old and toxic programming and making your mind understand that change equals growth and that growth equals excitement and happiness.

Bring awareness into your everyday life. Shift your focus from the things that frighten you to the things that excite you. Assume the best and expect only great things to happen.

Make your mind understand that pain doesn't come from change but rather from stagnating, from resisting change and from resisting life, from refusing to do the things that your truthful self wants you to do and from acting on daily habits and continuing to live your life on autopilot.

4. Life Is a Process of Becoming

Life is a process of becoming, a combination of states we have to go through. Where people fail is that they wish to elect a state and remain in it. This is a kind of death.

—ANAÏS NIN

We go through life to find ourselves, to become ourselves. Through every little thing we do, through every word we say and through every action we take, we are meant to discover more and more about our true selves, about our inner journey, our life path, and about the purpose and meaning of our own lives. And by embracing change and allowing ourselves to move from one state to another, from one place to another, we give ourselves permission to be who we really are. We give ourselves permission to explore, to discover and to constantly create wonderful new experiences for ourselves.

This is what life is really all about.

We are not trees. We are not meant to stay in one place forever. We are meant to move, to stretch, to grow and to constantly go on adventures into the unknown. And we can do this by putting our fears behind us, and by trusting that no matter how far we go, life will always take good care of us—because it will.

We are all here for a reason. Each and every one of us has a purpose to fulfill. We all have a unique and precious contribution to make to this world. And the more we let go of our resistance, of our fears, excuses and limitations, by leaving what's familiar behind and stepping into the unknown, the more we will be able to realize this truth and the easier it will be for us to contribute and to do the beautiful work that we came here to do.

5. You Will Fall Down, but It's Okay

What do you first do when you learn to swim? You make mistakes, do you not? And what happens? You make other mistakes, and when you have made all the mistakes you possibly can without drowning—and some of them many times over—what do you find? That you can swim? Well—life is just the same as learning to swim! Do not be afraid of making mistakes, for there is no other way of learning how to live!

—ALFRED ADLER

As you walk through life, you will fall down many times. You will fail and you will make mistakes, but that's okay.

Don't be afraid to make "mistakes." Don't be afraid to fail. Don't be afraid to fall and don't be afraid to make a fool of yourself. Have fun in all that you do. Make the best of every experience and every interaction life sends your way and choose to do all things from a place of love.

Always remember that life is a process of becoming and that through every painful and humiliating experience, and through every hurtful and heartbreaking interaction, you discover more about yourself and about who you truly are.

Make peace with the idea of failure and make peace with the idea of mistake. Waste no time on fear and choose to do all things from a place of love. For love is who you are and love is what you are made for. Always remember, as George Bernard Shaw famously said, that "a life spent making mistakes is not only more honorable, but more useful than a life spent doing nothing."

Chapter 6

GIVE UP BLAMING

We are taught you must blame your father, your sisters, your brothers, the school, the teachers—but never blame yourself. It's never your fault. But it's always your fault, because if you wanted to change you're the one who has got to change.

—KATHARINE HEPBURN

MY STORY

I moved to the U.S. in January 2007, to work in the food and beverage department at a four-star international hotel in Orlando, Florida, and build a new and better life with Stefan. Away from home and away from the life I was so accustomed to.

Stefan was so happy and excited. He was so eager to show me all the places he had been during his first trip. He wanted me to be happy, to feel comfortable and to realize that I had made a good decision by moving to the U.S. However, even though I really wanted to appreciate and enjoy the new life I was living, for some reason I just couldn't do it.

Taken out of my "nest" and away from my comfort zone, I started thinking more and more about how much I wanted to go back home and about how wrong I had been to listen to Stefan.

Because I was not able to adapt to the new environment and the new life I was living, it didn't take long until in my mind's eye I started seeing the life I had at home as being so beautiful, so magical and so perfect. I idealized it, and increasingly saw the life I was living in the U.S. as very unhappy.

I seemed to be feeling worse and worse with every passing day. I wanted to go back to my old life.

.   .   .

For weeks, Stefan and I treated each other with respect and kindness, but all of that eventually changed.

"Stefan, why did you force me to come here?" I bitterly told him one day, masking what I felt with a question.

"Can't you see how miserable I am in this place? Can't you see how unhappy I am?"

"I should've never listened to you. I should've just stayed back home in Romania."

"I made a huge mistake coming here and it's all your fault."

"I just want to go back!"

I never shouted at him, but as I felt the increasing pressure of the changes, I struggled. Without having the necessary skills to cope and adapt to our new environment, and without even realizing it, I started replicating my father's behavior, doing what my father knew best how to do: inflicting pain on those around him and blaming them for his own inner suffering. I started projecting my anger, frustration and inner turmoil onto Stefan, blaming him for how lost and unhappy I was feeling.

I just couldn't control myself. I couldn't make myself stop. I was no longer in charge of my thoughts, actions and behavior. My past programming was.

•   •   •

After a while, Stefan no longer wanted to spend much time together. He no longer enjoyed being around me. Acting cold and distant, he spent more time in front of the computer than with me.

As for me, feeling disconnected and neglected, I spent more and more time at work, immersing myself in job responsibilities, to forget about the pain I was feeling.

My manager, Danny, a man in his late twenties, and my supervisor, Lecsy, a woman in her thirties, were two positive and inspiring people. They were leaders who treated everyone with lots of love and respect.

They both saw in me things I did not know I had, making me feel as if I was a very valuable and worthy human being, capable of achieving great things.

It was the first time I had the privilege to call anyone my mentor.

Danny and Lecsy were the people who planted a seed in my mind that would later on help me discover more about myself and what I was really made of.

LESSONS IN LETTING GO

The best years of your life are the ones in which you decide your problems are your own. You do not blame them on your mother, the ecology, or the president. You realize that you control your own destiny.

—ALBERT ELLIS

For a long time, I believed that life was something that happened to me and that I had no say in it whatsoever. As a result, I started blaming outside circumstances for why my life was the way it was, thinking that I was never responsible for anything that was happening to me, that I was at the mercy of external circumstances.

I blamed my father for depriving me of love and nourishment; my mother for all the violence I had to go through while my father was alive, as well as for all the pain I had to endure after his death; my boyfriend for not making me feel as happy and as loved as I wanted to feel, and the world around me for being so cruel and unkind toward me.

I blamed everything and everyone, and as long as I continued to do so, I continued to feel like a powerless victim, and perpetuated my own suffering.

*   *   *

There is no peace in pointing the finger and making others responsible for how you feel and for what your life looks like. There is no peace in giving your power away to forces outside of yourself and making them responsible for the quality of your life. There is no peace in putting your life in other people's hands and expecting them to live it for you.

Even though our parents, our teachers, our friends, our boyfriends, our girlfriends, our life partners and the whole world might have steered us in the wrong direction through their ignorance and poor behavior, and even though at one point they might have deprived us of the respect, love and affection we deserved, it's our responsibility to take charge of our lives and steer ourselves in the direction we think we deserve to go. It's our responsibility to make ourselves feel worthy and loved, to remove ourselves from toxic relationships, places and experiences. And it's our responsibility to live our lives well, the way we desire.

> There is an expiry date on blaming your parents for steering you in the wrong direction; the moment you are old enough to take the wheel, responsibility lies with you.
> —J.K. ROWLING

Blaming is a waste of time and energy. It does no good. Not to you and not to those you are blaming. And the less time you spend blaming, criticizing and complaining, the more time you will have left to heal yourself, your wounds and your life.

If you continue to blame outside circumstances for the way you feel and if you continue to put your life in the hands of other people, you will continue to be at the mercy of other people and you will continue to be a victim of your circumstances.

Raina, a woman in her mid-thirties who has been reading my blog for more than a year, understands this very well.

Having lived with a very controlling and manipulative father, someone who was constantly telling her how to live her life, Raina grew up thinking that love equaled control, and that the men in her life always knew better how she should live. That's how she ended up in a relationship with a man who not only manipulated and controlled her, but was also living a double life. After being in a relationship with him for more than eight years, planning their future and talking about raising a family together, the moment Raina realized that their entire relationship was built on a lie, her love for him turned into hate. Her passion and dedication turned into blame, anger and resentment.

Not knowing how to deal with all that pain, for a year or so she nearly destroyed her health, her career and her entire life because of all the toxic thoughts and emotions that were piling up inside of her. But when she finally realized that all that blame, anger, hate and resentment was hurting her more than it was hurting him, she decided to stop. Instead of continuing to blame him for everything that happened, she decided to take back her power by assuming responsibility for the part she played in their failed relationship. She worked on giving up blame by forgiving not only him, but also herself, for allowing things to happen the way they did. Today, after being separated from him for nearly two years, Raina is living on her own terms, free from resentment and free from pain. She's happier than she's ever been.

Your life is yours to live. Your path is yours to walk on. But if you continue to cling to blame, you will continue to feel powerless.

By letting go of blame and by taking responsibility for everything that you feel and everything that you are, you will spend your life building beautiful things and crafting a happier future.

THE PATH TO "GIVING UP"

1. Take Inventory of Your Blame

Only by much searching and mining are gold and diamonds obtained, and man can find every truth connected with his being if he will dig deep into the mine of his soul.

—JAMES ALLEN

Take the time to look within, to reflect and to acknowledge that there is guilt, regret and blame present in your life. Take the time to acknowledge that you are holding on to something that is causing you to experience pain, anxiety and a lot of unhappiness.

Take inventory of whom you blame, why and for what.

Are you blaming your parents for not being there for you when you really needed them, for not encouraging you to become the person you once wanted to become and for imposing their beliefs and limitations on you?

Are you blaming yourself for not having the courage to do many of the things you wanted to do but didn't?

Are you blaming the world around you for not being more supportive and more loving toward you?

Are you blaming your partner for treating you poorly and for not loving you as much as you would want him or her to love you? For not making you feel happier?

Are you blaming the economy, the media, the society you live in or maybe the head of your own country for why your life looks the way it does?

Forgive them all. Be willing to make peace with your past and move on with your life.

Don't burden yourself with unnecessary thoughts, regrets and memories. Let go of blame and make room in your heart for peace and love to enter.

2. Play the "What If" Game

Take your life in your own hands, and what happens?
A terrible thing: no one to blame.
—ERICA JONG

What if you could go back in time and see it all happening the way you think it should've happened?

What if you used the power of your imagination to see how your life would've looked if you had done all the things you are now blaming yourself and others for your not doing?

What if you took the time to contemplate, to meditate and to imagine yourself being, doing and having all those things you now blame yourself and others for depriving you of?

What if you decided to see it all happening in your mind's eye and to discover whether that was really the life you were supposed to be living?

If you are willing to give this a try, find a quiet place where you won't be disturbed. Close your eyes and imagine yourself doing all the things you once wanted to do but couldn't.

Feel the feelings that come from having, doing and being all that you once wanted to be, do and have. See yourself surrounded by the people you would've surrounded yourself with and see your whole life unfolding in a completely different way.

Allow yourself to see it, to feel it all and to observe it all. Give yourself permission to discover whether that was really the life you were supposed to be living. And when you feel ready, ask yourself:

"Am I happy with what I have created?"

"Would I really enjoy living this kind of life?"

"Is this really me? Is this really my life?"

"Do I want to live this kind of life?"

"Am I ready to do all that it takes to live this kind of life?"

Take the time to really think about these questions. And know that if the life you saw yourself living is the life you wish to be living, you can always start taking the necessary steps to move yourself in that direction. But if the life you saw yourself living is not aligned with who you are at the moment and with how you see yourself living your life, all the more reason to give up blaming and focus on where you truly want to go now.

3. Take Back Your Personal Power

In life, you can blame a lot of people and you can wallow in self-pity, or you can pick yourself up and say, "Listen, I have to be responsible for myself."

—HOWARD SCHULTZ

The more you blame outside circumstances for what happened to you in the past and for what is happening to you in the present, the more unhappy you will feel and the harder it will be for you to change your current circumstances and improve the quality of your life.

When you blame outside circumstances for whatever you are feeling or aren't feeling, for whatever you have or don't have, you automatically become a victim of your circumstances and of all those people you are blaming. You give them power over you, making them seem like giants in comparison to you.

The past is long gone and it can't be undone, the future is out of our reach, and all that we have left is this moment. So why not use this moment to create the life you want to live instead of blaming outside circumstances for how unhappy you are? Why not use this moment to start crafting a better life for yourself?

You are not a victim.

You are not a victim. You never were and you never will be. But when you cling to blame, you can't help but perceive yourself as one.

You are a powerful being. You have within you all the strength, knowledge, confidence and wisdom necessary to leave behind all that is toxic in your life and craft a better, happier and more balanced existence for yourself. So give up on blame and choose to make peace with everything that happened to you up until this moment.

Give up on blame and start focusing on creating the happy, loving and harmonious life you truly deserve.

4. Release Your Burdens; Forgive Yourself

Take a walk through the garden of forgiveness and pick a flower of forgiveness for everything you have ever done. When you get to that time that is now, make a full and total forgiveness of your entire life and smile at the bouquet in your hands because it truly is beautiful.

—STEPHEN RICHARDS

Place your hands over your heart, take a few deep cleansing breaths and repeat these words to yourself:

In this moment, I give myself permission to release and let go of all the pain that I have been carrying with me for all this time.

In this moment, I choose to be free from blame, free from pain and free from resentment.

In this moment, I choose to open my heart fully and let love flow in and out of my life.

In this moment, I love myself, I accept myself.

In this moment, I choose to release and let go of all the pain from my heart, my mind, my body and my soul.

In this moment I choose to forgive. I choose to let go. I choose to be free.

Self-forgiveness is such a powerful thing, for it can heal your heart, making room for love to reenter your world, allowing you to reconnect with your inner being in a very deep and meaningful way and to feel the love, the peace and the bliss that is always present deep within you. Self-forgiveness helps you return to a place of peace and tranquility and it helps you look at yourself, your life and the world around you through the eyes of love.

When you forgive, you love, and when you love, you become ONE with your heart and soul. ONE with your own divinity and ONE with the world around you.

The more you forgive yourself for the mistakes of the past, for the pain you have inflicted on yourself and others, knowingly and unknowingly, by clinging to blame and by holding on to all kinds of toxic thoughts, behaviors and attitudes, the easier it will be for you to free yourself from the victim position you have placed yourself in for so long.

Chapter 7

GIVE UP COMPLAINING

People who never achieve happiness are the ones who complain whenever they're awake, and whenever they're asleep, they are thinking about what to complain about tomorrow.

—ADAM ZIMBLER

MY STORY

If before I moved to the U.S. Stefan was the center of my universe and the love of my life, once we moved, all of that started to change.

Not knowing how to deal with life's many challenges, I started to rely more and more on him. And before I knew it I was 100 percent dependent on him. I took my hands off the steering wheel and expected him to lead the way, to meet all my needs and desires and to make my life feel complete.

I didn't know how relationships were meant to be strengthened and how love and support were meant to be expressed. And because of that I did what I best knew how to do. I did what I had seen my father doing to us. I pointed the finger and made Stefan responsible for all the bad things that I was experiencing and all the inner pain that I was feeling.

"Why did you bring me here?"

"This hot, sticky and humid weather is driving me crazy. I feel like I'm suffocating."

"When I'm outside I'm too hot, when I'm inside I'm too cold . . ."

"I have no air! I can't live like this."

"And the food . . . This food here is horrible. It has no taste."

"How can I live like this? How can I be happy when nothing seems to be going right?"

"Why are things so different?"

"What is wrong with this place? And what is wrong with you?"

"You used to care about my feelings, but now you don't. You don't even want to spend time with me anymore. I spend more time with these people from work than I do with you. They seem to care about me more than you do."

And that's how I would spend most of my days: arguing, crying, screaming and yelling at Stefan, calling him names and doing my best to hurt him as much as I myself was hurting. I thought that it was his job to make me feel happy and loved, not mine.

. . .

At work, it was a different story. I felt quite fortunate to be paid good money for something that I enjoyed doing.

But the fun wasn't going to last long. Because after only six months in Orlando, Florida, after six months of working at the hotel, we were about to find out that we could no longer extend our contracts. We had to move to Chicago, Illinois, and work there.

"I don't want to go," I kept telling my boyfriend. *"I want us to stay here. Please, find a way for us to stay here."*

Once again it felt like I was being forced to leave it all behind, to get out of my comfort zone and step into the unknown.

LESSONS IN LETTING GO

Complaining not only ruins everybody else's day, it ruins the complainer's day, too. The more we complain, the more unhappy we get.

—DENNIS PRAGER

Complaining, just like blaming and criticizing, sucks us dry. It keeps us in dark places, and it continues to feed this false idea that our lives will never get better until outside circumstances start to change. But the truth is that it's not the outside world that determines how we feel on the inside, but rather how we feel on the inside that determines how we perceive the outside world.

If you're happy and at peace with yourself, and if you know the reason for your existence and the purpose of your life, you have no interest in blaming, criticizing or complaining. Why? Because you're too busy loving, living and enjoying your life.

It's those who feel lost, who have no sense of direction and who can no longer remember what their path in life is who go around projecting their unhappiness into the world. It's those who have disconnected from their own inner peace and who can no longer feel the abundance of love that flows from their hearts who can't seem to find a way to be at peace with the world around them.

Jason, whom I have connected with through my blog, shared with me his personal experience about giving up complaining and negativity.

Ever since he was a young adult, Jason always seemed to have a reason to complain about everything that was going on in his life. He complained about his health, his family, his relationships, about the economy, about the weather, about his boss, his neighbors, and so on. No matter how much his friends, family and colleagues would try to encourage him, empower him and cheer him up, wanting him to look on the bright side of things, nothing really worked. It was only after his friends and family started avoiding him, no longer wanting to be in the presence of his negativity, that he decided to give up complaining and start looking for reasons to love and appreciate life. It wasn't an easy lesson to learn, but it was worth it.

Life treats us the way we deep down inside expect to be treated, constantly giving us the things we feel worthy of receiving. And if we don't like what we see, how we are being treated, if we are not happy with the things we are receiving, we shouldn't complain. Instead, we should just change the way we perceive things.

We should just adjust our attitudes and behaviors toward every experience and every interaction life sends our way. Because only by doing so will we find the strength, the wisdom and the patience to live our lives like alchemists, transforming all our difficulties into opportunities, our wounds into wisdom and our own darkness into light.

THE PATH TO "GIVING UP"

1. Understand Why People Complain

If you took one-tenth the energy you put into complaining and applied it to solving the problem, you'd be surprised by how well things can work out . . . Complaining does not work as a strategy. We all have finite time and energy. Any time we spend whining is unlikely to help us achieve our goals. And it won't make us happier.

—RANDY PAUSCH

According to Will Bowen, the author of *A Complaint Free World*, there are five reasons people complain:

First, because of the need for attention. People want to be noticed and they use complaining as a way to "bond" with others.

Second, because complaining removes the responsibility

from our shoulders. Pointing the finger seems easier than assuming responsibility and actually doing something about the things that bother us.

Third, because of pride and competitiveness. We tend to think that pointing out the things that are wrong with others will show the world how much better we are. We complain about those who are "less" capable than we are.

Fourth, to exercise power. As Bowen observed, "People often complain to incite others to abandon an alliance and switch to their point of view, and/or build support and power by focusing on what's wrong with another's position." We manipulate our words to manipulate others.

Fifth, to excuse poor performance. When something doesn't go as planned, we start to complain, placing the blame on someone else but never on ourselves.

It's very important to understand the reasons behind our constant need to complain. Because once we do, we can begin to let go and take the necessary steps toward achieving inner peace and happiness.

2. Recognize the Price You Pay for Complaining

> People won't have time for you if you are always angry
> or complaining.
> —STEPHEN HAWKING

When you have little or no control over your thoughts, when you believe all the fearful, toxic and negative thoughts that run through your mind, you can't help but point the finger. You can't help but complain about everything and everyone.

Complaining is a dreadful addiction that creates a false sense of separation between you and the world around you. It keeps you from connecting with yourself and the world at a deeper level. It keeps you stuck in a place where outside circumstances seem to always control you and sabotage your happiness, health and well-being.

The more you complain, the further and further away you move from those around you but also from your true essence, from that part of you that is always loving and always connected to everything and everyone.

You are an example for those you love. You are a role model for your children. You are an example for your family members, your friends, the people you work with and for every person you come in contact with. Through your words and actions you can either inspire and draw people to you or discourage and push people away. And if the time you spend with them is wasted on blaming, complaining and criticizing the world around you, chances are that they won't learn much from you. Chances are that they will not enjoy being in your company, and as time goes by they will want to spend less and less time in your presence.

Every word you speak and every action you take impacts you and those around you in a positive or not so positive way. Through your words, actions and behaviors you either create a happy world for you to live in or an unhappy world. That's how powerful you are.

3. Change Your Attitude, Transform Your Life

> There were people who went to sleep last night, poor
> and rich and white and black, but they will never wake
> again. And those dead folks would give anything at all
> for just five minutes of this weather or ten minutes of
> plowing. So you watch yourself about complaining.
> What you're supposed to do when you don't like a
> thing is change it. If you can't change it, change the
> way you think about it.
>
> —MAYA ANGELOU

In his book *Man's Search for Meaning* the Austrian neurologist
and psychiatrist Viktor Frankl, a survivor of the Holocaust,
talks about the importance of having a positive attitude and
outlook on life even in the midst of great pain and sorrow:
"The one thing you can't take away from me is the way I choose
to respond to what you do to me. The last of one's freedoms is
to choose one's attitude in any given circumstance."

You have the power to choose a positive attitude in any
given circumstance and not to be enslaved by all the pain,
suffering and unhappiness that surrounds you. Everything
can be taken from you but one thing: the last of the human
freedoms—to choose your attitude in any given set of circumstances, to choose your own way.

It's true that there is a lot of pain, fear, injustice and ugli-
ness in the world, but it's also true that there is plenty of love,

beauty, wealth and kindness, people who act in compassionate and loving ways toward others, people who have learned to use every experience life sends their way, whether good or bad, and turn it into a positive, inspiring and empowering opportunity.

If there is something in your life that you don't like, do something about it. Take the necessary steps to change your current circumstances. And if you can't change them, change your attitude.

Change the way you look at whatever happens to you and around you. Look for the lessons, look for the meaning. Use every experience to propel yourself farther in life and not to get stuck and become even more unhappy.

Embrace a loving attitude. Accept things as they are. Don't allow your problems to become bigger than you. Don't allow your complaints to keep you from looking for solutions. Don't allow your mind to keep you stuck.

4. Ask Yourself, "What Do I Love?"

For the first time in my life I saw the truth as it is set into song by so many poets, proclaimed as the final wisdom by so many thinkers. The truth—that Love is the ultimate and highest goal to which man can aspire. Then I grasped the meaning of the greatest secret that human poetry and human thought and belief have to impart: The salvation of man is through love and in love.

—VIKTOR E. FRANKL

Take the time to ask yourself:

"What do I love?"

"What do I want?"

"What are the things that make me happy?"

"What do I appreciate about myself, my life, the people and the world around me?"

"Do I want to find the solutions to my problems or do I only want to complain?"

"What do I love?"

What do you love? What do you really, really love?

What do you love?

If you spend too much time focusing on the problems, looking for reasons to get offended, you will lose yourself in the process and you will forget about the things that truly matter. You will forget about the things that have the power to resurrect your soul and bring love back into your life.

Your life won't get better by itself. Your life will get better when you yourself get better. By giving up complaining, by focusing on that which you love and want to have in your life, and by taking the necessary steps to move yourself in a better direction, you will create a more beautiful and happier life for yourself and those you love. And there will be much less for you to complain about.

Chapter 8

GIVE UP THE LUXURY OF CRITICISM

When we judge or criticize another person, it says nothing about that person; it merely says something about our own need to be critical.

—UNKNOWN

MY STORY

I cried for days, not wanting to leave behind the new life I had created in Orlando, and not wanting to abandon my friends. But eventually, after eight months of living in Florida, we packed our stuff, said goodbye to our friends and drove all the way to Chicago in my boyfriend's car.

Not long after we arrived in Chicago, once again I began to feel the same discomfort, anger, pain and resentment I'd felt the moment I first arrived in the U.S. But this time, the feelings became more intense, violent and aggressive, and worst of all, much more mutual between Stefan and me.

Now, instead of trying to keep it to himself, my boyfriend began yelling back:

"I'm so sick and tired of your whining, just shut the hell up and let me breathe!"

"Leave me the hell alone!"

And I would immediately start to cry.

I wanted him to acknowledge me and my suffering. But he couldn't do it anymore. He had his own inner pain to deal with.

.   .   .

Growing up in an abusive environment led me to assume subconsciously that love equaled drama and that drama equaled love. You see, in the three years that Stefan and I spent in the U.S., I did my best to "love" him in the same way I saw my father "love" my mom: by making his life feel like a living nightmare and making him regret the day he fell in love with me.

Our whole experience in the U.S. was supposed to bring us closer together, to unite and help us connect in a deeper and more meaningful way, to make our relationship stronger and our love flourish. But none of these things happened.

Sadly, in the two years and a few months we lived in Chicago, we managed to completely damage the pure, innocent and loving relationship we'd once had, and to exhaust any remaining love we had for each other.

As time went by, Stefan and I went from soul mates to cell mates, trapped on the inside by our own fears, insecurities and attitudes of criticism, with the keys to freedom in our hands but with us unable to use them.

We became people who were living in the same house, under the same roof, not because they wanted it, not because they were in love, but because they thought they had no other choice, because they were "forced" by the circumstances they were in to continue to eat together, sleep together and pretend they were together.

After almost three years of living in the U.S., in the fall of 2009, after many ugly fights, a lot of pushing and pulling, screaming and yelling, we both agreed that it was best for us to go back to Romania, back to where it all started.

LESSONS IN LETTING GO

Any fool can criticize, condemn, and complain but it takes character and self-control to be understanding and forgiving.

—DALE CARNEGIE

People grow together with love and appreciation, not blame, judgment and criticism. Relationships flourish when there's respect, understanding and support between the people involved, and they perish when those things are missing. But I didn't know that. I had no idea how relationships were meant to work and how life was meant to be lived.

It took me quite some time until I finally understood that relationships aren't about making an unhappy person happy, nor are they about making an unloved person feel loved. Relationships are about sharing the love and happiness that is already present within you with each other, growing, improving and evolving together, both emotionally and spiritually.

For all the time we spent in the U.S., I was so blinded by my pain that I couldn't see what I was doing. I couldn't see that through my constant nagging and toxic behavior I was poisoning not only myself but Stefan as well.

I criticized him and I criticized the whole world for not loving me, for not treating me the way I hoped to be treated, not knowing that they weren't the source of my unhappiness, I was.

The same thing happened to Daniel, another reader of the PurposeFairy blog. Ever since he was a little boy, Daniel had constantly been criticized by his parents. He grew up with the impression that criticizing himself and those around him was a normal thing to do. When he got married, he criticized his wife every day, always focusing on the things she did "wrong" and on the things she needed to change so that they could be happy. It wasn't until his wife threatened to file for divorce, tired of his nagging and criticism, that he finally opened his eyes and understood that if he wanted to save his marriage, he needed to learn how to love and appreciate his wife, not to criticize everything he thought was "wrong" about her. That was the wake-up call he needed. Daniel and his wife managed to heal their relationship and are now instilling in their daughters the importance of mutual respect and care.

．　·　．

But it is not what I am saying that is hurting you; it is that you have wounds that I touch by what I have said. You are hurting yourself. There is no way I can take this personally.

—DON MIGUEL RUIZ

How we experience the world is largely a projection of who we ourselves are. Our relationships and our lives are nothing but a construct of our thoughts, ideas and beliefs.

If there's inner turmoil, unease, pain and past wounds that are not yet healed, consciously or unconsciously we will project all those negative things outside ourselves, and we will attract into our lives the people, places and experiences that will continue to feed our inner shadows and darkness.

Our job is not to criticize what others are doing. Our job is to focus our energy on healing, accepting, loving and embracing all that we are. Because the moment we make peace with ourselves, we also make peace with all those things, people, places and experiences that once caused us to feel hurt, unloved and neglected.

It is only by letting go of the pain we harbor within us and only by filling our hearts with love and compassion that we can see the world as it really is. Only by loving ourselves can we love the world around us, and only by no longer criticizing ourselves will we stop criticizing others.

THE PATH TO "GIVING UP"

1. Recognize That We Are All One

A human being is a part of the whole called by us universe, a part limited in time and space. He experiences himself, his thoughts and feelings as something separated from the rest, a kind of optical delusion of his consciousness. This delusion is a kind of prison for us, restricting us to our personal desires and to affection for a few persons nearest to us. Our task must be to free ourselves from this prison by widening our circle of compassion to embrace all living creatures and the whole of nature in its beauty.

—ALBERT EINSTEIN

On the surface we might all look very different from one another, but at the core level we are all the same. At the core level we are all ONE, connected with one another in a very deep and powerful way. At the core level we are essentially the same, all members of one human race. There is no separation except the separation we create in our minds because of our attachment to fear.

This isn't an idealistic sentiment. When President Bill Clinton announced the results of the Human Genome Project on June 26, 2000, he noted that upon examining the discovered elementary building blocks in the DNA sequences, scientists had concluded that we truly are in essence the same and members of one larger family. We truly are all ONE.

There is much more to life than what meets the eye. There's more to each and every one of us than our fearful and judgmental minds want us to believe.

There is much more to life than what meets the eye.

Don't be fooled by appearances. Seek to understand, accept and embrace the oneness of things. Don't let your fearful mind strengthen this false idea in your head that who you are is better or worse than everyone else, that who you are is separate from everyone else.

2. Make Peace with Your Own Darkness

Why do you look at the speck of sawdust in your brother's eye and pay no attention to the plank in your own eye? How can you say to your brother, "Let me take the speck out of your eye," when all the time there is a plank in your own eye? First take the plank out of your own eye, and then you will see clearly to remove the speck from your brother's eye.

—MATTHEW 7:3–5

Look around you, at all those people, events and places that you find distasteful, different, ugly and unworthy, and see if you can recognize yourself in them. Every fault you find in others touches a denied weakness in yourself. If the things you see on the outside bother you, it's only because they reflect back at you the things that are already within you.

Every fault you find in others touches a denied weakness in yourself.

The world is our mirror, reflecting back at us the things that are already within us—the things that are tormenting us, the things we haven't yet found a way to make peace with and the things we are constantly rejecting and hiding from ourselves.

Bring awareness into your life. Give as much attention to your thoughts, feelings and reactions as you give to those things, people and experiences that cause you to hold on to judgment and criticism.

Pay close attention to your reactions, and whenever you catch yourself projecting your own darkness, your own pain and your own suffering onto those around you, with a smile on your face, silently repeat these words to yourself:

"I am better than this. I can do better than this."

And choose to do better.

Give up the need to judge and criticize not only those around you but also yourself. Learn to look for the good in people and also in yourself. Accept and make peace with your own darkness so that you can accept, embrace and make peace with everyone else's darkness.

Heal every part of you that's in need of healing. Make peace with your imperfections, your fears, doubts and insecurities, and you will be at peace with the whole world.

3. Put Yourself in Their Shoes

Who are you to judge the life I live? I know I'm not perfect—and I don't live to be—but before you start pointing fingers . . . make sure your hands are clean!
—BOB MARLEY

Deep down inside we are all the same. We all want to love and be loved, we all want to be happy and to share our own happiness with those we love. No sane person wakes up with the intention to hurt other people or to make their lives harder.

Everyone's doing the best they know how to do. Everyone has their own story, their own reasons for doing the things they do. And even though at first sight it might look like some people are just horrible human beings, if you look deep within them, beyond their words, actions and behaviors, chances are that you will see more than that.

We are all shaped differently by our environment, by the people we spend most of our time with, by our friends and families, and also by the education we received while growing up. But even though on the surface it might look as if we're all very different, if we can look beyond the surface and if we can put ourselves in the shoes of those we feel the need to criticize, we might discover that all those differences that we first perceived are nothing but illusions, and that deep down inside we are all the same.

Whether it's your partner, your children, your boss, the head of your country or just a stranger you meet on the street, instead of impulsively reacting to what they're saying and doing, put yourself in their position instead. Walk in their shoes for a little while, and imagine what it feels like to live the life they are living, to make the choices they are making. See if you can give up the luxury of criticism and embrace a compassionate attitude instead.

4. Embrace a Compassionate Attitude

People hurt others as a result of their own inner strife and pain. Avoid the reactive response of believing they are bad; they already think so and are acting that way. They aren't bad; they are damaged and they deserve compassion. Note that compassion is an internal process, an understanding of the painful and troubled road trod by another. It is not trying to change or fix that person.

—WILL BOWEN

Nobody's perfect. We all have flaws, we all have internal conflicts to deal with, and we all have many hidden wounds that we're desperately trying to hide or heal. And even though at times, consciously or unconsciously, people might project their darkness, their pain and their suffering onto you and onto the world around them in toxic and unhealthy ways, it doesn't mean that they are bad people. It only means that they still haven't found a way to love themselves as much as they want the world to love them.

Give love to all and seek to criticize none.

Treat everyone according to the Golden Rule. Do unto others as you would have them do unto you. Talk to and about others in the way you would have others talk to and about you. Treat the world around you in the same way you would like to be treated: with respect, love, kindness and compassion.

Speak kindly of everyone, including yourself. Seek to understand all things and all people. And if you don't like what other people are saying or doing, refrain from rejecting, labeling and harshly criticizing them.

Don't look for things to criticize, look for things to appreciate, both in yourself and in everyone you come in contact with. Trust that everyone is exactly where they're supposed to be, doing the best they know how to do, learning and growing at their own pace. Give everyone permission to live the best they know how, and pray that they will do the same for you.

Chapter 9

GIVE UP LIVING YOUR LIFE ACCORDING TO OTHER PEOPLE'S EXPECTATIONS

He who trims himself to suit everyone will soon whittle himself away.

—RAYMOND HULL

MY STORY

I was only twenty-five years old when I went back to Romania. I felt disconnected and out of place. I no longer felt like I belonged there.

Many of the people my age were already college graduates with master's degrees, with jobs, married, or preparing to get married, and I felt as though I was far behind them.

I didn't seem to have any of the things people my age were expected to have.

Without a boyfriend, without a job, without a university degree and without any plans for the future, it wasn't long until I started drowning in regret and feeling like a total failure.

"I am twenty-five years old and I haven't done anything with my life."

"I should never have gone to the U.S."

"I should've stayed home and finished my university."

"Everyone else is living a normal and happy life except me!"

Every day, I put more and more pressure on myself, constantly repeating to myself that I had failed in life. It obviously did me no good.

.   .   .

Eventually, I gave in to social pressures and expectations, and rejoined university, despite hating it.

I sat in the classroom, listening to dry lectures, while disconnected and unable to understand a word the professors were saying.

And if that wasn't enough, people around me bombarded me with all kinds of questions and uninvited comments about my life:

"Lumi, why did you make the mistake of coming back home? Aren't you scared that you're not going to like it here?"

"What happened between you and Stefan? You two were perfect for each other. Are you going to get back together? Most people your age are already married and have families."

"Do you think you're going to find a good job since you don't have a college degree yet? I don't think they'll hire you . . ."

As a result, I desperately started looking for jobs, even though I didn't yet feel ready to do so; I started looking for a new boyfriend even though I was still heartbroken because of what happened between me and Stefan; and I started doing all kinds of meaningless and shallow things just because that's what people expected a girl my age to do. I thought that if I finally started living my life like everyone else said I should, I was finally going to be happy—"normal" like everyone else.

LESSONS IN LETTING GO

I do my thing and you do your thing. I am not in this world to live up to your expectations, and you are not in this world to live up to mine. You are you, and I am I, and if by chance we find each other, it's beautiful. If not, it can't be helped.

—FRITZ PERLS

For too long, I had believed that I was supposed to live my life according to other people's expectations and "sensible norms," that I was supposed to obey, to follow the crowd, and play by the rules.

It took me more than twenty-five years to finally understand that I wasn't supposed to live my life in a way that felt right for others, but rather in a way that felt right for me.

There's nothing more painful than trying to live your life the way everyone expects you to live it—betraying your own soul just so you can please the world around you.

I love how Iyanla Vanzant puts it: "How you treat yourself is how you treat God. Because you are the representation of God in your life . . . Which means you're putting other things and other people ahead of God in your life."

It's true that our families, friends and the many people around us expect a lot of things from us, but it's also true that we have our own heart to please and our own life's purpose to fulfill. And if we waste our lives trying to be whatever everyone expects us to be, we can no longer honor the relationship we have with our own heart and soul, with our inner divinity, and we can no longer fulfill our own destiny.

. . .

My dear friend Vishen Lakhiani was raised in an Indian family in Malaysia. Like many Indian teens growing up in the nineties he was pushed by family, teachers and society to be an engineer. Engineering, particularly computer engineering, was seen as a sign of success. Vishen worked hard for good grades, and got into the University of Michigan. He slogged through lecture after lecture on Computer Engineering and Math. But it was painful. He disliked the course work. Inside he felt more like an artist. He studied Photography and got As. He studied Drama and Theatre and loved being on stage. But his Engineering and Math classes only earned him Bs and Cs. Still he pressed on.

When he was close to graduating, he was offered a job at Microsoft in Seattle. Less than 1 percent of interviewees ever get a job there. Everyone was proud of Vishen. But after eleven weeks working at Microsoft he was so miserable and bored he left the company. He went back to university to complete the degree, but he knew he never wanted to be a computer engineer. He had taken a path in life based on other people's expectations.

Upon graduating, Vishen worked for a nonprofit, he traveled the world, he tried his hand at many different jobs. He even became a meditation instructor for a while. Everyone he knew told him it was a silly career and no one would take him seriously. Plus, what type of money could you make teaching meditation? Yet all the dots connected. He ended up starting a major meditation destination site. Today, Mindvalley.com employs two hundred people and counting. Vishen is wealthy beyond his wildest dreams. And he says he feels like he hasn't worked hard for many years because every day brings him joy doing what he loves.

So you see, life needs you to be YOU—the unique being that you were born to be, nothing less.

THE PATH TO "GIVING UP"

1. Choose Temporary Discomfort over Long-Term Resentment

It doesn't interest me if the story you are telling me is true. I want to know if you can disappoint another to be true to yourself; if you can bear the accusation of betrayal and not betray your own soul.

—ORIAH MOUNTAIN DREAMER

Too many of us are living a life that is not our own. Don't let the expectations of others distract you from your own path. Don't put your happiness on hold. Give up living your life according to other people's expectations and start living life in a way that feels right for you instead, even at the risk of "offending" those around you.

Why choose long-term resentment over temporary discomfort? Why betray yourself, your own needs and desires just because other people expect you to? Always remember that you can only give to others as much as you give to yourself, and if you yourself aren't happy and at peace with yourself, you won't be able to make other people happy either.

Seek to do the things that bring YOU joy, meaning and happiness. Make yourself a priority.

Learn to listen to your own inner voice and guidance more than you listen to the loud noise of those around you.

> Be as good to you as you want to be to God in order to be of service to others in the world . . . It's self-full to be first, to be as good as possible to you. To take care of you, keep you whole and healthy. That doesn't mean you disregard everything and everyone. But you want to come with your cup full. You know: "My cup runneth over." What comes out of the cup is for y'all. What's in the cup is mine. But I've got to keep my cup.
>
> —IYANLA VANZANT

The irony is that when you follow your own path, others will respect you more in the long run. Set your own boundaries and show the world what you are truly made of.

2. Set Your Boundaries

> Daring to set boundaries is about having the courage to love ourselves, even when we risk disappointing others.
>
> —BRENÉ BROWN

People treat you the way you teach them to treat you, the way you allow them to treat you. By constantly saying yes to others when deep down inside you actually mean to say no, and by constantly putting your own needs and desires aside just so you can fulfill the needs and desires of those around you, you are sending the wrong message to yourself and to everyone else. Through your approval-seeking behavior, you tell yourself and the whole world that who you are is not enough and that you need other people's approval in order for you to feel whole, loved and validated.

Learn to say no when you feel like saying no and yes when you truly feel like saying yes. Let people know what you tolerate and what you don't.

Don't be afraid to speak your truth. Don't be afraid to put your own needs above the needs of everyone else. Don't be afraid to "betray" others just so you can honor and be true to yourself.

Work on rebuilding and strengthening the relationship you have with yourself. Focus on your own happiness, health and well-being. Honor your integrity. Treasure your divinity. Set your own boundaries. Honor yourself, your needs, your dreams and desires. Be true to yourself. Follow your heart and intuition. Treasure your authenticity. Fully embrace who you are. Let the world see the real you. Let people love you for who you truly are and not for who they expect you to be.

3. Free Yourself

Learn to . . . be what you are, and learn to resign with a good grace all that you are not.

—HENRI-FRÉDÉRIC AMIEL

Ask yourself:

"How would I feel if I were free?"

"How would I feel if I started living life my own way and no longer according to how others expect me to live?"

If you try to be what the whole world wants you to be, putting your needs aside and trimming yourself to suit everyone else, you will never be truly free.

Look within yourself. Ask your soul to lead the way, to guide you and to show you the way back to yourself and back to being the unique and wonderful being you were born to be. You owe it to yourself to live life in a way that makes you happy, in a way that makes you feel free.

4. Honor Your Authenticity

Always be yourself, express yourself, have faith in yourself, do not go out and look for a successful personality and duplicate it.

—BRUCE LEE

Most of us were raised to believe that being obedient and living our lives according to how other people expect us to live is the perfect way to get love and approval. We believe that if we do what other people expect us to do, we will be liked and we will find long-lasting happiness. But that's not really what will bring us happiness.

Life isn't about pretending. Life isn't about being what others expect you to be and living the way they expect you to live. Life is about being the unique and authentic being you were born to be. It's about walking on the unique and meaningful path you were intended to walk on.

True happiness comes from being yourself, from honoring who you are and from living your life in a unique and authentic way.

If you follow the crowd, you will get no farther than the crowd. If you want your life to be meaningful and unique, you have to have the courage to do things that the majority of people don't have the courage to do. You have to have the courage to honor your authenticity and live your life the way it feels right for you, not for them.

Give up living your life according to other people's expectations and choose to live it your way instead. Don't waste your gifts and talents. Don't deprive the world around you of the beautiful and meaningful work you came here to create.

5. Seek to Live Purposefully

Everyone has been made for some particular work, and the desire for that work has been put in every heart.

—RUMI

Anthony Robbins once said that "Quality questions create a quality life. Successful people ask better questions, and as a result, they get better answers." And that's why it's very important for you to ask yourself these questions and many others of this kind:

"What is it that I have to offer?"

"What can I do better than anyone else?"

"What is my deepest and most powerful desire?"

"How do I want to be remembered by my friends, my children and my family?"

"Is there purpose in my life?"

"Am I happy with the life I am now living?"

Seek to honor your inner voice and intuition more than you honor the loud voice of those around you. Live your life on purpose. Don't do things because the world expects you to do them but rather because they make sense to you. Do them because something inside of you is asking you to do them.

In the wise words of Rumi, "Start a huge, foolish project, like Noah . . . It makes absolutely no difference what people think of you."

Chapter 10

GIVE UP YOUR
SELF-DEFEATING SELF-TALK

We have to learn to be our own best friends because
we fall too easily into the trap of being our own worst
enemies.

—RODERICK THORP

MY STORY

I had always been a bit of a loner, for better or worse. Often it was in those moments of solitude that I was extremely harsh toward myself, beating up myself with excessive self-defeating self-talk.

I remember when I was younger, in the years that followed my father's death, my mom would often say to me:

"Dani, go outside. Go get some fresh air. You spend too much time alone in the house. It's not normal. Go outside and play with the other kids."

But I rarely did. I felt I was far behind most of the kids in my class when it came to grades and intelligence levels. I believed that I wasn't as smart as they were. I felt that I needed to spend more time in the house studying and less time outside playing. And the same thing happened once I got back from the U.S.

After a few months of trying very hard to integrate myself back into the environment I had been in, I decided to do what my heart was asking me to do—isolate myself like I used to do when I was a little kid and focus on studying for university and reading as many books as possible.

It did me both good and bad.

After I was done reading the personal development book Danny, my friend and manager, gave me while I was in Orlando, I became very interested in reading and learning more about how to use the power of the mind to change old habits and create a happy life for yourself. So I started reading a lot of books in the field of psychology, psychoanalysis, personal development, spirituality, religion, anthropology and more. I felt like there was something I needed to discover and that all those books were going to help me do just that. That was the good news.

The bad news was that when I locked myself in the house for weeks, not wanting to talk to anyone and not wanting to see anyone, the self-defeating self-talk returned with intensity and nonstop tenacity. I felt like I needed to be alone with myself, away from everyone to face myself, know myself, heal myself and educate myself. I thought that if I could be alone, away from all those I believed were the cause of my pain, I was going to feel better. But I was wrong, because I couldn't get away from my own internal self-defeating self-talk. I hated my own company.

"Do you realize how pathetic you look hiding here from the whole world?" a nagging and hateful voice inside my head kept saying.

"How long do you think you will be able to sit here alone in your miserable presence? No wonder you try to hide from the world around you. It's because nobody likes you, right? What's there to like? Just look at yourself! You're nothing but a loser. You're twenty-five years old and you haven't done anything with your life."

"Why do you think your father never loved you? And why do you think Stefan left you? Because you're worthless and nobody will ever love you!"

"You think that just by reading some stupid books on how to be happy, how to cleanse your mind, heal your life and become a better person, you will actually be happier and live a better life?"

"You're so naive!"

"Stop making a fool of yourself! Put those books aside and accept the fact that you are a poor little loser and that you will always remain a loser!"

Ouch.

I could feel my whole body being poisoned by all the toxic thoughts, by all the self-hate and anger. And no matter how hard I would try to stop myself from hurting myself, I just couldn't do it.

And so, because I didn't know what else to do, I started praying.

"God, please make this pain go away. Make it stop! I can't han-

dle any more pain. It's too much for me. Too much . . . Please, God. Please help me! Make it all stop. Make it all end . . ."

Even though God never seemed to answer any of my prayers, and even though it felt as if whenever I was talking to God I was in fact talking to the walls, after that night, for some strange reason, I felt a strong urge to write, to start a blog and to write about all that I was going through, all that I was thinking and feeling.

I resisted that urge at first, thinking that I had no idea how to write, or what to write about, but because the urge to write kept "bothering" me, I eventually gave in. And that's how my blog, PurposeFairy.com, was born. In short, writing became my therapy, an outlet for turning the energy of my self-defeating self-talk into a ritual for positive self-improvement and self-growth.

LESSONS IN LETTING GO

You and I are not what we eat; we are what we think.
—WALTER ANDERSON

Until not so long ago, I never really stopped to think about whether I had anything to do with how unloved I felt.

I never really stopped to think whether my internal dialogue, my toxic, negative and repetitive self-defeating mindset had anything to do with the quality of my emotions, or with how people were behaving toward me.

Thinking that it was always their fault, and thinking that I was nothing but their victim, I failed to realize that I too was responsible for how poorly life was treating me, and that I too was to blame for how unhappy and unloved I was feeling. It took me many years to see how wrong I was.

*   *   *

A toxic mind has the power to create a toxic life. It has the power to sabotage our happiness, our relationships and our lives, and it has the power to constantly re-create the same painful experiences, either in the same places with the same people, or with completely different people and in completely different places.

Having been raised in a toxic environment, I did my best to re-create those past experiences in my relationship with Stefan and in my relationships with others around me—and with life itself.

It wasn't until life "forced" me to spend a lot of time alone with myself, away from all those external things, people and experiences I thought were making me feel unloved, unworthy and unhappy, that I was finally able to understand that the only reason all those people, things and experiences were present in my life, and the only reason they had so much power over me, was that I was allowing it.

When you yourself think that you're unworthy of love, happiness and affection, and when you yourself use all kinds of negative, toxic and self-defeating words to describe yourself, you can't help but expect those around you to do the same. And through your actions and behaviors, you will do what it takes to make them treat you as poorly as you believe you deserve to be treated.

Amir Ahmad Nasr, whom I mention in the acknowledgments at the end of this book, is a close friend and a fellow author. In January 2014, he suddenly had to leave his comfortable life in Southeast Asia behind because his book was banned there. He fled to Canada for political asylum. While he was there, we would Skype, and he would confide in me how bitter he felt. He was no longer the cheerful and defiant guy I knew in Malaysia, but someone who now engaged in lots of self-defeating talk.

Eventually, though, he realized that his behavior was not doing him any good. It only served to make him feel worse. Many months later, he admitted, "I wish I had been kinder to myself those early months. I couldn't help but feel like friends I respected were progressing with their lives, and that I had lost, and that my efforts to create some change were for nothing. Little did I know that those individuals I was comparing myself to were going through their own personal hardships. If only more of us engaged in constructive self-critique instead. Truthfully, we should all be kinder to ourselves and to each other."

It all starts with you. It starts with how you think about yourself, with how you talk to, and about, yourself, and with how you expect to be treated by those around you and by life itself. And once you give up your self-defeating self-talk, once you purify your own thoughts and your heart, the world around you miraculously gets purified as well.

THE PATH TO "GIVING UP"

1. As You Think So Shall You Be

If you realized how powerful your thoughts are, you would never think a negative thought.

—PEACE PILGRIM

It is said that we have around sixty thousand thoughts per day and that most of these thoughts are negative. We think the same thoughts over and over again, telling ourselves the same sad and depressing stories day after day, failing to realize that in order to create different and better lives for ourselves and those we love, we need to start telling ourselves different and better stories.

Thoughts have great power—creative power. With every thought you craft and shape your life. The life you are now living is the result of all the thoughts you have thought up until this moment. Your present level of self-esteem, your confidence and your sense of self-worth were determined by all the thoughts you have ever thought and all the words you have ever said to yourself.

The quality of your present relationships, the way you look at the world, your beliefs and limitations, your fears and insecurities—they are all the result of the many thoughts you have kept affirming to yourself. You are what you think.

You are what you think.

For as he thinketh in his heart, so is he.

—PROVERBS 23:7

If the mind is pure and if the thoughts you think are healthy, positive and empowering, no matter how many horrible things happen to you, and no matter how poorly those around you treat you, you will always find a way to use those experiences to propel yourself higher in life and not get caught up in the drama and become their victim. But if your thoughts are negative, toxic and self-defeating, you will continue to be at the mercy of those painful experiences.

2. Put Your Mind Under the Microscope

As you think, you travel, and as you love, you attract. You are today where your thoughts have brought you; you will be tomorrow where your thoughts take you.

—JAMES ALLEN

Pay close attention to the thoughts you think and the words you speak. Notice the feelings and emotions your internal dialogue is causing you to feel. Know that if your thoughts are making you feel good, if love flows through you and if you feel centered, peaceful and connected with yourself and the world around you, it means that your thoughts come from a place of love, authenticity and integrity. However, if your thoughts are making you feel unloved, unworthy, anxious and afraid, and if you feel pain and discomfort in your body, your thoughts are most likely coming from a fearful place.

Constantly question your toxic, negative and repetitive self-defeating mindset.

Whenever negative thoughts pop in your mind, take a few deep cleansing breaths and ask yourself:

"If I am made of love and made to love, are any of these thoughts real?"

"If love is the only thing that's real and fear is just an illusion, is there any truth in this negative and self-defeating self-talk?"

Take your mind off of autopilot.

Learn to recognize when your thoughts are aligned with your loving and authentic self and when they are not. Learn to differentiate between the thoughts that come from a place of fear and the thoughts that come from a place of love—between the thoughts that are meant to keep you in the dark and the thoughts that are meant to bring you back to light. And choose to trust only those thoughts that are meant to get you back on your life path and back to living your life from a place of love, integrity and authenticity.

3. Act Yourself into a New Way of Thinking

If you want a quality, act as if you already had it. Try
the "as if" technique.

—WILLIAM JAMES

If you don't yet have a role model, someone who inspires and
empowers you to become a better person and live a happier and
more harmonious life, see if you can find this person somewhere out there. It really doesn't matter if you find this person
in books, games, stories or real life experiences. It really doesn't
matter if they are alive or not, if you have ever met them or not.
All that matters is for you to find this person and then see if you
can model their behavior, thoughts and attitudes.

Whenever you catch yourself going down a rocky path,
whenever you sense that your mind is starting to bully you, using negative and self-defeating words to describe you and your
life, ask yourself:

*"If I were X or Y [the name of a person you admire], how would
I respond to this situation?"*

"What would be the thought that would run through my mind?"

*"What would be my attitude, my behaviors and my internal di-
alogue?"*

Having a positive role model will help give you courage,
confidence and a sense of direction. And it will make this process of mind cleansing and mind detox more exciting and a lot
easier.

4. Spend Time Alone in Silence

God's one and only voice is silence.
—HERMAN MELVILLE

Silence is a precious gift. In that space between our words is where we find ourselves. When the mind is quiet, when there are no thoughts and no words to be said, we can hear our own heart talking to us. We can hear our own soul and our own intuition communicating to us.

When we allow ourselves to be quiet, to breathe in and breathe out, without the need to force ourselves into saying another word or thinking another thought, that's when we can hear our inner voice, our heart and intuition. That's when we can experience our own divinity, our own beauty and perfection.

Take time from your busy schedule to be alone with yourself in silence, to quiet your mind and to free yourself of all those negative, fearful and toxic thoughts, to get in touch with that side of you that doesn't need words in order to communicate.

Take time from your chaotic life to contemplate and to meditate; to familiarize yourself with your innermost thoughts and feelings; to know yourself, to accept yourself and to learn how to love yourself; to empty your mind of all thoughts and to be at peace.

Each night, before you go to bed, spend at least ten minutes meditating. Release and let go of all the thoughts you have about what happened during the day and all the thoughts you have about the things you need to do when you wake up. Release and let go of all thoughts of worry, stress and fear.

Let your mind rest, renew, refresh and rejuvenate itself. Let yourself feel the peace, stillness and tranquility that is always present deep within you.

When you wake up in the morning, repeat this process. But this time, meditate on the feelings you would like to feel within you all throughout the day. Envision how you would like your day to unfold, and feel the joy that comes from living each moment with awareness and a deep sense of love and gratitude.

The more you do this, and the more time you spend alone in silence, the more your mind will be cleansed and the easier it will be for you to think thoughts that come from a place of love.

5. Rebuild the Relationship You Have with Yourself

Love yourself—accept yourself—forgive yourself—
and be good to yourself, because without you the rest
of us are without a source of many wonderful things.
—LEO F. BUSCAGLIA

Let go of the need for perfection. Let go of all thoughts of self-judgment, self-blame and self-criticism and work on improving your internal dialogue. Work on improving the relationship you have with your loving soul and authentic self.

Look for things to appreciate about yourself, about your life and about those you love. Take time to be alone with yourself, to know yourself and to love yourself, to align your mind with your heart and to craft your life from a place of pure love and high integrity.

Give yourself permission to do nothing; to spend more time in solitude; to think less and to feel more; to love more and to fear less; to express yourself in creative ways, to spend less time criticizing and judging yourself and more time accepting, nourishing and loving who you are.

Surround yourself with beauty and authenticity. Immerse yourself in thoughts that make you feel good, in activities that make you feel alive. Spend your time with people who bring out the best in you, and give yourself permission to be happy.

Offer yourself the love and respect you truly deserve—not tomorrow; not in a year; not when you will lose those extra pounds; not when you will be happier; not when you will have a mate; not when you will have more money; not when you will have more friends; not when you will be more beautiful and not when all your problems will cease to exist; but now!

Ask yourself all kinds of questions about yourself and about your life. Get interested in who you are. Get interested in learning more about what your soul longs for and about what your heart truly desires. And whenever you catch yourself falling into the trap of using negative, toxic and self-defeating words to talk to yourself, take a few deep cleansing breaths and then ask yourself:

"If I had a friend who spoke to me this way, would I still be friends with this person?"

Talk to and about yourself in the same way you would talk to and about someone you love and adore. Treat yourself with the same respect, love and appreciation with which you would treat someone you love and adore. Be kind and loving toward yourself.

Always address yourself with words that are positive, empowering, uplifting and inspiring. Talk to yourself in the same way you would want a dear friend to talk to you. Seek to make the relationship you have with yourself the most beautiful, most loving and most important relationship in your life.

Give to yourself as much as you would want others to give to you. Think of this as the "reverse golden rule." And know that when you do so the world around you will start replicating your behavior.

Chapter 11

GIVE UP CONTROL

The reason many people in our society are miserable, sick, and highly stressed is because of an unhealthy attachment to things they have no control over.

—STEVE MARABOLI

MY STORY

In every instance of transformation, as you have been reading so far, the transformative insight was always one that led me to letting go, surrendering and giving up, in the best sense possible.

And perhaps out of all the self-sabotaging habits of thought and behavior, the one that's far too common is our desire to control aspects of reality that are actually beyond our control. Things like events, people and, yes, even ex-boyfriends.

Even though I knew that Stefan and I were toxic for each other and would not go back to having the pure, healthy and loving relationship we'd had in the beginning, I couldn't stand to be alone. You know what they say, misery loves company, and I desperately needed to share my misery with Stefan.

"We are like cat and mouse. We literally almost drove each other mad while we were in the U.S. Why would you want to go back to that?" Stefan would say to me whenever I tried to convince him that we should go back to being a couple. *"Can't you see we're better off separated? Can't you see how much better things are now that we're just friends? It will all be okay eventually. Just be patient, okay?"*

But I didn't want to be patient. I didn't know how to be patient. And all I kept thinking was that I had to get him back. I was obsessed with this idea of us getting back together, and despite his rejections, I just couldn't accept the truth.

I kept calling him, I kept texting and checking up on him, acting as if he were my property. I wanted to make sure I had full control over him, over the situation and over everything he was doing. I honestly believed that if I could do so, he would never find somebody else and eventually he would find his way back to me.

But then in the spring of 2011, after I had spent more than one year desperately trying to control his every move, the one thing I feared the most happened.

Stefan got out of his car, started walking toward me where we had agreed to meet on that spring day, and as soon as I saw the look on his face, I immediately knew something was different.

The smile on his face, the sparkle in his eye—they looked

so familiar. I knew I had seen them before. And before I could get my thoughts in order, my mouth blurted out the realization.

"Oh my God! You're dating someone!"

The moment I said those words, his facial expression changed immediately, as if he could anticipate what was coming at him, and before he could say anything, I was in tears and a shambles.

He no longer loved me.

At that moment, I knew that if I didn't find a way to let go of my unhealthy desire to control Stefan, my past would continue to haunt me. I had to find a way to heal my wounds.

LESSONS IN LETTING GO

Be not angry that you cannot make others as you wish them to be, since you cannot make yourself as you wish to be.

—THOMAS À KEMPIS

Over and over I have tried to control how my life unfolded, how people perceived me and how my boyfriend treated me, among so many other things many of us too often attempt to control.

I thought that this was what I had to do in order to keep my life from falling apart, in order for me to find love, peace and happiness. But the more I tried to control everything and everyone, and the more I insisted on making things go my own way, the unhappier I became and the more chaotic my life seemed to get. So I had to stop.

Seeing that I wasn't getting any healthy and positive results through my obsessive and controlling behavior, I eventually decided to surrender. To let go and just relax into life. I decided to release control—no longer going against the flow, but with it. And the irony is that the moment I decided to release control, the moment I decided to stop trying so hard to make my life work, to make people like me and to make them love and approve of me, that's when everything started to fall into place. That's when my life started to follow its natural course—taking me places I had never dreamed of going, meeting people I had never dreamed of meeting and doing things I had never believed myself capable of doing.

*   *   *

So don't be frightened, dear friend, if a sadness confronts you larger than any you have ever known, casting its shadow over all you do. You must think that something is happening within you, and remember that life has not forgotten you; it holds you in its hand and will not let you fall. Why would you want to exclude from your life any uneasiness, any pain, any depression, since you don't know what work they are accomplishing within you?

—RAINER MARIA RILKE

Another dear friend of mine, Tharyn, shared with me how he gave up control and allowed life to take care of everything for him. He had just gotten back to his home in the U.S. after working in Southeast Asia for nearly two years. Upon arriving home, he had no solid plans and began searching for what to do next. However, in less than a month, his search became an obsessive and anxious bad habit. He kept trying to control all the circumstances of his next steps, and yet the harder he tried, the more he seemed to struggle and the more difficult his life seemed to get.

After many weeks of anxiety and uncertainty, he decided to surrender. He thought of his previous winding path, and all the miracles that had happened on the way when he allowed things to flow naturally. He made the leap to give up control and put his trust in life once more, to let things work themselves out. Then, out of nowhere, an opportunity arose that took him to a magnificent place he had never known existed. When he let go of the outcome he thought he wanted, he let in the outcome he really needed. Which made him realize that life happens the way it's supposed to happen, not the way we think and try to make it happen.

Even though things might not always go the way we want them to go, and even though life might not always give us the experiences we want to have, it doesn't meant that life isn't offering us the experiences we NEED to have—the experiences that are beneficial for the evolution of our consciousness, the growth of our own souls and the expansion of our whole beings.

Life knows a lot more than we do, because life is a lot wiser than we are. And even though our minds might try to convince us that we need to control everything and everyone, and we need to make sure that things always go our own way, the truth of the matter is that life is meant to be lived, not controlled; people are meant to be loved, not controlled; feelings are meant to be felt, not controlled. And by giving up control and allowing life to guide us, we will be able to experience, understand and know this truth.

THE PATH TO "GIVING UP"

1. Whatever You Need, Life Will Supply

Ask, and it will be given to you; seek, and you will find; knock, and it will be opened to you. For everyone who asks receives, and the one who seeks finds, and to the one who knocks it will be opened.

—MATTHEW 7:7–8

In the movie *The Shift*, Wayne Dyer talks about how for the first nine months of our existence, everything we needed for our growth and development was provided to us, naturally and effortlessly.

While we were in our mother's womb, we didn't have to fear, control, stress over and worry about what color our eyes were going to be or how our organs were going to develop. We simply surrendered and trusted that everything was being taken care of for us. We trusted the wisdom of life and we trusted ourselves. But as we grew older, constantly hearing that the world around us was a fearful and hostile place, and being exposed to painful and unhappy experiences and circumstances, we slowly but surely began to drift away from that trust. We forgot about our true nature and we began to think that we were all alone and helpless.

Our lives aren't meant to be difficult, but we make them so by constantly doubting ourselves and interfering with the natural flow of life.

> *Our lives aren't meant to be difficult,
> but we make them so by constantly
> doubting ourselves and interfering
> with the natural flow of life.*

When you think that you are all alone in this world and that you have to work very hard to achieve happiness, you can't help but live in fear. You can't help but try very hard to control everything and everyone. You can't help but desperately try to control how your whole life unfolds. And the more you try to control everything, the more everything seems to get out of control.

Allow life to supply all your needs, not according to your

limited expectations, but according to life's unlimited resources and riches. Trust that just as everything you needed in those first nine months of your life was being offered to you, naturally and effortlessly, everything you need for the rest of your journey here on this planet will also be provided to you in the same beautiful, natural and effortless way the moment you release your worries, give up the need for control and put your trust in life.

2. Trust Your Inner Wisdom

There is a universal, intelligent, life force that exists within everyone and everything. It resides within each one of us as a deep wisdom, an inner knowing. We can access this wonderful source of knowledge and wisdom through our intuition, an inner sense that tells us what feels right and true for us at any given moment.
—SHAKTI GAWAIN

In the same way we trust the sun to shine and give us light; in the same way we trust that our breath, our eyes, our heart, and all our organs will continue to function—in the exact same way we need to learn to trust our inner wisdom, and also the wisdom of life.

We all have an inner GPS to lead us in the direction we are meant to be going. By getting out of our own way and by giving up the need to control, we allow ourselves to act upon our heart's desire and to do the things that our soul needs us to do.

Learn how to develop, listen and trust this inner voice. Learn to trust your heart and to follow intuition. Trust that there is a natural flow to life, and choose to go with it, not against it.

Instead of believing every fearful thought your mind wants you to think, choose to listen to what your heart has to say instead. Choose to trust your feelings more than you trust your fearful thoughts. Know that if there's tension and anxiety present within you, you are disconnected from your authentic self. And if you feel peaceful and at ease, if love flows through you, it's because you have chosen to relax into your true nature, to allow life to guide you and to trust that it will take good care of you, because it will.

3. Do Your Work, Then Step Back

Can you deal with the most vital matters by letting events take their course? Can you step back from you own mind and thus understand all things? Giving birth and nourishing, having without possessing, acting with no expectations, leading and not trying to control: this is the supreme virtue.

—LAO TZU

Think of yourself as a farmer. Faithfully scatter your seeds (wishes) across the field of life, water them down whenever needed and leave the rest to nature.

Allow life to do what life needs to do.

Don't try to force things into existence. Don't worry. Don't hurry. Just trust the process. Trust the wisdom of life and trust that everything is happening exactly the way it's supposed to happen, because it is.

Do your part then step back.

Allow things to unfold naturally without you trying to control everything that happens to you. Allow life to take its natural course, to take you where it needs to take you and not where you think it should take you. Trust that maybe life's plans for you are better than your plans.

Let go of fixed plans, rigid beliefs and concepts about how life should unfold, about how things should be, about how people should behave, and keep your mind open to what is.

If things don't happen the way you want them to happen, based on the image you had in your head, let it go. Trust that maybe things weren't meant to happen the way you wanted them to happen and that maybe something better is waiting for you not too far from these so-called failures and mistakes.

Give up the need to adjust life according to your own script and instead work on allowing life to guide you. Learn to go with the flow of life and you will end up exactly where you need to be—not where your fearful self thinks you should be, but where your soul knows you belong.

Surrender to what is. Make peace with this idea that people are made to be loved. That things, places, experiences are meant to be enjoyed. That feelings aren't meant to be controlled and that life is meant to be lived, not controlled. Give up your need to always control everything that happens to you and around you—situations, events, people, etc. Whether they are loved ones, coworkers, or just strangers you meet on the street—just allow them to be. Allow everything and everyone to be just as they are. Allow life to be as it is.

Chapter 12

GIVE UP THE NEED
TO ALWAYS BE RIGHT

The need to be right—the sign of a vulgar mind.

—ALBERT CAMUS

MY STORY

By May 2011, writing had become a regular self-empowering habit that helped me grow wiser and stronger. Blogging became a source of strength and, as I shall reveal, indirectly also became a source of new frustrations, because I fell into the trap of needing to always be right.

On the bright side, blogging helped me get my mind off Stefan. For hours, I sat in front of my laptop, constantly writing new posts, watching all kinds of inspirational videos, taking notes, and reading all sorts of materials to help ease the pain I was feeling.

Despite the inner hurting, I had faith that one day things were going to get better for me and that I would finally get to live the peaceful, happy and balanced life I dreamt of.

I had no idea when or how that was going to happen, but I was beginning to feel it more and more within myself. And so, with every day that went by, I felt the urge to write more and more, to write about what I was going through, what I was feeling and the many ways one could bring happiness and peace back into one's life. And the more I did that, the more I blogged, the better I started to feel and the less time I seemed to spend obsessing about Stefan and his new girlfriend.

It was actually during that time that I wrote my extremely viral blog post "15 Things You Should Give Up to Be Happy," shared more than 1.2 million times on Facebook, and which this book is based on. Little did I know that it was going to be through writing and blogging that I'd heal my past wounds, as well as live a life of joy and freedom beyond what I'd ever dreamed possible.

Funnily enough, however, after some time, even though my blog became a tool for self-growth, it also began attracting criticisms from people I knew who read it.

In short, most of my critics were trying to convince me that what I was doing was nonsense and that I needed to find a better and more "productive" way of spending my time.

"What's up with this blog of yours?" they often asked me with a critical tone.

"Since when did you become a writer and start believing in this nonsense you're writing about?"

"All this new age crap is only meant to manipulate people. Why would you write about something like that?"

"This isn't new age crap," I would reply, feeling slightly irritated, before launching into a heated argument with the critic. *"Do you even know anything about personal development? Have you read any books in this field? I'm sure you haven't!"*

Almost every discussion I had about my blog ended up in an argument about who was right and who was wrong, and made me feel bitter and resentful toward the critic in question.

With the exception of my best friend Anca, almost everyone who knew about my blog was constantly trying to tell me that I should stop.

They all seemed to have something against me, forever telling me that I had no right and no expertise to talk about the things I was talking about, that I was feeding people illusions. And the more they would insist that it was all nonsense and a way to manipulate people, the angrier I'd get and the more I would try to convince them they were terribly wrong.

I wanted people to believe me. I wanted them to agree with me. I was more interested in proving myself right than in being happy, and because of that, I failed to realize that it really didn't matter whether they believed me or not. It really didn't matter if they thought they were right and I was wrong.

What mattered was what I thought of myself, and the hundreds of emails from readers who found inspiration and solutions in my words.

LESSONS IN LETTING GO

Say not, "I have found the truth," but rather, "I have found a truth." Say not, "I have found the path of the soul." Say rather, "I have met the soul walking upon my path." For the soul walks upon all paths. The soul walks not upon a line, neither does it grow like a reed. The soul unfolds itself, like a lotus of countless petals.

—KHALIL GIBRAN

I used to think that things were either black or white, good or bad, beautiful or ugly, right or wrong, and that whenever someone perceived reality differently from what I was perceiving, it was my responsibility to argue with them and prove that I was right and that they were wrong.

Throughout the time we spent in the U.S., Stefan and I would often engage in all kinds of arguments over silly things, and because we both saw our own point of view as being the right one, we would each try very hard to convince the other that the other was wrong, turning a silly argument into a huge fight.

We were more preoccupied with being right and making the other person wrong than we were with loving, supporting and caring for each other. And even though at that time I couldn't see how much this need to always be right was hurting our relationship, as soon as I got back to Romania, and as soon as I started reflecting on everything that had happened between us, I began to understand that it wasn't really worth it.

* * *

Our minds are evolutionarily wired to look out for trouble, and whenever you fall into the trap of arguing with others over who is right and who is wrong, that's exactly what you will find—trouble.

We are all the same in essence, and yet different in identity. We each have a unique set of DNA and we each perceive the world in different ways.

There is nothing healthy in arguing with someone over who is right and who is wrong. There is nothing healthy in damaging the quality of our relationships and causing a great deal of stress and suffering for ourselves and for others, just so we can be right and label the other person wrong.

Arguing with people over who is right and who is wrong is nothing but a waste of time and energy. Life isn't about doing things that make sense and feel right for others. Life is about doing things that feel right and make sense for us, and allowing others to do the same for themselves.

THE PATH TO "GIVING UP"

1. Know Your Worth

No tree has branches so foolish as to fight amongst themselves.

—NATIVE AMERICAN PROVERB

When you know who you really are and where your real value and self-worth come from, you don't waste time trying to defend yourself and your opinions, alienating those who see the world differently than you do. You accept the world as it is, and even though you might not agree with how others live their lives, you understand that we are all doing the best we know how to do. And when we know better, we will do better.

On the other hand, when you live your life from a fearful place, when you take your sense of worth, your identity and your value from external things, you will find yourself investing a lot of time and energy arguing with people over who is right and who is wrong.

When you believe every toxic thought that runs through your mind, being right feels very important because it gives you a false sense of power, security and control. These small victories place you in an imaginary state of superiority, making you feel smarter and more valuable than those you proved wrong. But none of them have anything to do with who you truly are.

The real you, who you are underneath it all, knows that at the core level we are all connected with one another in a really divine and powerful way, and because of that, it understands the futility of arguing with another human being over who is right and who is wrong. It knows that once you argue with another you are, in fact, arguing with yourself. And so, it seeks to love. To be one with everything and everyone without judging, without competing and without trying to prove anything to anyone. It seeks to live in peace and harmony with the whole world.

2. Treasure Your Relationships

> Words have the power to both destroy and heal. When words are both true and kind, they can change our world.
>
> —BUDDHA

If you have reached the point in your life and your spiritual evolution where you can see the big picture, where you understand that being kind is better than being right, choose to let it go.

Who cares if you are right if in the process you caused someone else to feel unworthy and unloved? Who cares if you prove to the whole world that you are right and they are wrong if in this process you damage or even destroy your relationships with those around you?

Fighting over who's right and who's wrong can cause lasting damage to relationships, and to others' sense of self-worth. Take a step back and remember what's most important. Don't let your ego get in the way.

Don't let your ego get in the way.

Be an example for those around you. Demonstrate to everyone you come in contact with, through your words, attitude and behaviors, that you treasure your relationships more than the need to be right all the time, that happiness and peace of mind are a lot more important to you than winning arguments over who is right and who is wrong. Make peacefulness your highest priority. Let nothing and no one disturb your peace of mind.

3. Choose Kindness

Choose to be kind over being right and you'll be right every time.

—RICHARD CARLSON

Many of us can't stand the idea of being wrong, and will risk ending relationships or causing a great deal of stress and pain, for ourselves and for others, to prove we're right. It's just not worth it. Whenever you feel the "urgent" need to jump into a fight over who is right and who is wrong, ask yourself this question, as posed by Wayne Dyer: "Would I rather be right, or would I rather be kind?" And choose to always be kind.

Remember that the most important thing in life is to enjoy who you are—to love yourself, to love the people around you and to accept, embrace and love everything that life sends your way. Strive to accept that not everyone will agree with you. Practice tolerance, love and acceptance instead of constantly arguing with others and trying to prove that you are right and they are wrong. Put love first.

Choose to be kind and you'll have more happiness and peace in your life.

Listen to what others have to say with an open mind and a loving heart. Be open and willing to understand their point of view, and by doing so, not only will you help lessen the resistance you feel toward them and toward their ideas, but you will also learn to look at things from a new perspective.

Every human being wants to be understood and acknowledged. Every human being wants to feel that who they are matters and what they say is valued by those around them.

Give people what they're looking for. Give them the love and approval they need and long for.

Seek to treat everyone as you would like to be treated. Instead of immediately reacting to what people have to say and instead of trying very hard to convince them that they are wrong and you are right, see if you can understand their point of view. See if you can understand them first before trying to make them understand you. See if you can give them your love and attention instead of listing all the reasons why you think they are wrong and you are right. Choose to be kind over being right and see how much better that will make you feel.

Chapter 13

GIVE UP THE NEED
TO IMPRESS OTHERS

A truly strong person does not need the approval of
others any more than a lion needs the approval of sheep.

—VERNON HOWARD

MY STORY

It was an ordinary day outside, but inside myself, what used to
feel ordinary for years—confusion, shame, anger—had stopped
being so. Instead, my inner life was becoming stronger by the
day, and that's when it happened. That's when I discovered the
company that would take me to the paradise islands and trop-
ics of Southeast Asia, and that would also bring me face-to-face
to confront a new toxic need: the need to impress others.

It was in my last year of university that I stumbled upon

Mindvalley, a global personal development digital publishing powerhouse based out of Kuala Lumpur, Malaysia, and led by the man who was fast becoming a hero to me, the company's founder and CEO, Vishen Lakhiani. I was instantly drawn to the brand and what it stood for.

The timing was perfect. Soon to be equipped with my university degree, and already equipped with my strong fascination for personal development and spirituality, I suspected it was going to be very easy for me to get a job with Mindvalley. And I was right.

Out of nearly a hundred applicants, I got selected because of my great passion and love for personal development, and on August 30, 2011, I set foot in Malaysia and Mindvalley's HQ in a moment that absolutely felt surreal.

.   .   .

As soon as I walked through the door, after arriving directly from the airport, Vishen, the man whose work I so loved and admired, was standing in front of me. And with a big smile on his face, and arms wide open ready for a hug, he said to me:

"Welcome to Mindvalley. This is where you will be working from now on."

It was in that moment that I felt I had to make Vishen proud of me and to prove to him that he had made a great choice by hiring me.

.   .   .

Right from the start, I was eager and excited to begin working in my new role, and to learn as much as possible. I felt blessed to be paid for something I had so much fun doing, and as the months went by, I got promoted along the way.

More and more, I also admired Vishen for his leadership style, his knowledge, the way he treated everyone, his humility, and his sense of humor.

In the midst of all of that, it became quickly obvious that he was the superstar of his own company, and I could see how everyone was trying hard to be noticed by him. And in time, I started doing the same thing.

It wasn't a good idea, because pretty soon the intention I regularly put into my work began to change. It became more about impressing Vishen and less about my love for my craft and for personal development.

I mistakenly believed that by doing this I'd feel happier and more accomplished, but to my surprise, the more I chased love and approval from outside of me—from people I was trying to impress—the worse I felt.

LESSONS IN LETTING GO

Be yourself. If you water yourself down to please people or to fit in or to not offend anyone, you lose the power, the passion, the freedom and the joy of being uniquely you. It's much easier to love yourself when you are being yourself.

—DAN COPPERSMITH

As you've read in previous chapters, for far too often throughout my life I lived under the impression that who I was was never enough—never good enough, smart enough, beautiful enough, worthy enough, and so on. I had this belief that everyone around me was worthy and valuable except me. As a result, I tried very hard to copy other people's behaviors, thinking they knew better, and hoping that by doing so, I too was going to become worthy and valuable, just like they were.

It wasn't until I began to understand that my worth came from how I felt internally and not from how many people praised me externally that I finally began to let go of the need to impress others and to focus on loving and impressing my true self instead. And the irony is that the more I stopped trying so hard to impress those around me and get their approval, the more love and approval I seemed to receive.

· · ·

We live in a world that teaches us to look for external love and approval—a world that teaches us that in order for us to feel truly happy, we have to please those around us by behaving in certain ways, and by surrounding ourselves with all kinds of expensive and shiny things. As a result, "We buy things we don't need with money we don't have to impress people we don't like," as Dave Ramsey has so aptly observed.

Your job here on earth is not to spend your life impressing those around you. Your job is to be yourself, authentically and unapologetically, to live your life in a way that makes sense for you—to love yourself and honor yourself more than you care about impressing those around you.

As long as you continue to think that you need to chase people's love and approval, you will be their prisoner.

THE PATH TO "GIVING UP"

1. The Only Person You Should Aspire to Impress Is Yourself

Why do you think the old stories tell of men who set out on great journeys to impress the gods? Because trying to impress people just isn't worth the time and effort.

—HENRY ROLLINS

You are the most important person in your life, and before going out of your way trying very hard to make everyone love and approve of you, you need to make sure that you yourself love and approve of you. You need to make sure that you yourself are impressed with the way you live your life and with the way you behave toward yourself and toward those around you.

In a world where we are led to believe that we have to try very hard to impress everyone around us, dare to be different.

Seek to live a life that not only looks good on the outside, but also feels great on the inside.

Never put other things and other people ahead of you in your life. Never fall into the trap of thinking that who you are is not good enough and that in order to be loved and approved by others you have to start pretending to be something you are not. Treat yourself with the love and respect you truly deserve.

Make the relationship you have with yourself the most important relationship in your life and seek to always honor who you are even if that won't make you too popular among other people. Always remember that it's not the world you should aspire to impress, it's yourself. Your heart, your soul and your inner divinity. They are the ones you should aspire to impress, since they know better than anyone else what is best for you.

2. You Alone Are Enough

> The greatest difficulty is that men do not think enough of themselves, do not consider what it is that they are sacrificing when they follow in a herd, or when they cater for their establishment.
>
> —RALPH WALDO EMERSON

So many people live under the impression that who they are is not good enough and that in order for them to become whole and complete, in order for them to receive love and affection from those around them, they have to try very hard to impress everyone and they have to behave in ways that aren't always aligned with who they truly are.

Believe it or not, love and approval aren't things you're meant to chase after. Love and approval aren't things you're meant to beg from those around you. Love and approval are meant to come your way effortlessly from simply being yourself, from honoring who you are and from living your life with integrity.

All the happiness, love and approval you need and desire will never be found in trying to impress the people around you. It can only be found by looking within and by recognizing that who you are is enough, whole and complete, and that you don't need anyone or anything to make you feel this way.

You were born whole and perfect, and who you are underneath it all never stopped being whole and perfect. You really don't need to add anything to your life, or get any more love and approval from those around you, in order for you to feel this way. You already are enough.

You already are enough.

So why look outside yourself for something that is already within you? Why beg for love from those around you when there's an abundance of love within you, when within you lies all the love, appreciation, approval and affection you need and desire? In you, not outside you.

Leave behind your old ways of doing things and instead of chasing outside yourself for all the things you think are lacking from your life, start looking within yourself. Because only by doing so you will eventually realize that you alone are enough!

3. It's Called Self-Worth, Not Others' Worth

> Let the world know you as you are, not as you think
> you should be, because sooner or later, if you are pos-
> ing, you will forget the pose, and then where are you?
> —FANNY BRICE

Your value doesn't come from how much stuff you have, how shiny it all is or how much you paid for it. It doesn't come from how many people like you; it doesn't come from how much money you make or from how big your house is, nor is it determined by any other external factors.

Your value and true worth come from being the unique, precious and loving being that you were born to be. Your true value comes from the fact that you were once born into this physical world and that you are now living and breathing on this beautiful planet. That's where your true value comes from.

You are a valuable and worthy human being not because of how your life looks externally, but because of who you are internally.

Never get your sense of worth from outside yourself. Never fall into the trap of thinking that who you are is not enough and that you need other people's approval, love and validation in order to feel that you're of value. Never allow external things, places, people and circumstances to determine or tell you how much you're worth. It's called self-worth, not others' worth.

4. An Original Is Worth More Than a Copy

You were born an original. Don't die a copy.

—JOHN MASON

You and I know that an original is worth more than a copy. And when you live your life from a place of integrity and authenticity, focusing on being the best version of yourself, and sharing who you truly are with the rest of the world, that's when you begin to shine and that's when people start being drawn to you effortlessly.

Authenticity is what we all treasure, what we all value, and those who live in an authentic way attract the love and admiration of those around them in a very easy and natural way. We impress people by being a first-rate version of ourselves instead of a second-rate version of everyone else.

You weren't born to blend in. You weren't born to hide your true beauty, power and perfection from those around you. And you definitely weren't born to copy the behavior of those around you in the hope that by doing so you will become more impressive in their eyes. So strive to be true to yourself at all times.

You weren't born to blend in.

Live your life from the heart and always stay true to your life path and your values. Embrace your own authenticity. Embrace your uniqueness.

Stop trying so hard to be something that you're not just to make others like you and start just being yourself. Because the moment you stop trying so hard to be something that you're not, the moment you take off all your masks, the moment you accept and embrace the real you, you will find that people will be drawn to you, effortlessly.

Chapter 14

GIVE UP LABELS

When you don't cover up the world with words and labels, a sense of the miraculous returns to your life that was lost a long time ago when humanity, instead of using thought, became possessed by thought.

—ECKHART TOLLE

MY STORY

Before my article "15 Things You Should Give Up to Be Happy" went viral in April 2012, I was regular Luminita, the "Author Liaison" person promoted to "Product Development Creative Lead" at Mindvalley. These labels didn't have a strong charge to them. But after my viral blog post, things changed.

Thousands upon thousands of emails, comments and messages from people all over the world poured into my life. People of all ages wrote in to thank me for the work I was doing, and encouraging me to never stop writing. New hires at Mindvalley came to me, asking if I was the PurposeFairy and expressing how they read my blog with their friends back in their home countries.

With all that attention, it wasn't long until I started to identify myself with what I was doing.

In my mind, I was no longer Luminita, the girl who was working in Mindvalley. I was now the PurposeFairy. I was the blogger who had written the "most viral personal development article in the history of the Internet," whom everyone seemingly wanted to interview and talk to. The girl who knew what happiness was really all about and who was "wise beyond her years." And that became my label, my new identity, one which now carried a certain image and set of expectations.

.   .   .

Soon I felt like I was supposed to embody all the qualities that the PurposeFairy stood for, and whenever I would catch myself thinking a negative thought, whenever I would find myself in a stressful situation, and whenever I would behave in a way that wasn't aligned with how the PurposeFairy was supposed to behave, I would immediately try to suppress my "inappropriate" feelings and behaviors.

"I am the PurposeFairy now. I can't be stressed. I shouldn't think negative thoughts and I shouldn't have bad days."

"PurposeFairy is always happy and I need to do my best to be happy all the time."

Without me even realizing it, I had placed myself in a box, thinking that because I was someone who was writing and sharing her ideas—her knowledge and insights about life, happiness and purpose—I was supposed to skip many of the stages and lessons I still had to learn, to instead become this final, perfect "product."

Because I was putting so much pressure on myself, constantly trying to censor and keep myself from thinking, feeling, and from being myself, I was quickly forgetting that PurposeFairy was something I was moving toward; she was someone whose traits, qualities, wisdom and values I was learning and was going to embody in time through practice, through trial and error, and through experiencing life with its many ups and downs. I certainly was not going to do it by placing myself in a box and trying very hard to stay there.

LESSONS IN LETTING GO

He who stands on tiptoe doesn't stand firm. He who rushes ahead doesn't go far. He who tries to shine dims his own light. He who defines himself can't know who he really is. He who has power over others can't empower himself. He who clings to his work will create nothing that endures. If you want to accord with the Tao, just do your job, then let go.

—LAO TZU

The use of labels creates a veil in front of our eyes, impairing our sight and causing us to see the world as either black or white, good or bad, rich or poor, worthy or unworthy, and then treat everyone according to the values we give to each label.

Ever since I can remember I have tried so hard to become one with the many labels that were constantly being placed on me, by those around me and by myself, thinking that it was my responsibility to honor those labels and live my life according to the instructions written on the many "boxes" I was constantly being placed in. As a result, I suffered a great deal.

It wasn't until I started putting a lot of pressure on myself by constantly trying to censor and keep myself from thinking and feeling, from being who I really was, that I finally realized that my place wasn't in a "box" and that all the labels in the world would never really summarize who I truly am.

. . .

So many people identify themselves with their past, their job, their physical appearance, the money they make, the things they have, their social status, their religion, the country they were born in, with a disease they may have, and the many other labels that are constantly being placed on them by themselves or by those around them. And because of that, they fail to realize that these rigid labels and categories have nothing to do with who they truly are.

Iulian, my sister's fiancé, understands this truth better than anyone else. When he was seventeen years old, he was diagnosed with stage 4 cancer. The doctors told him and his parents that he only had a few months to live, and because he saw the doctors as authoritative figures who knew everything about his health, he gave up on all the ideas he had about who he really was, and became a cancer patient instead. For the next six months, this was the only label he carried around with him. But one day, through a beautiful and miraculous conversation he had with one of his doctors, he realized that cancer was something he had, not something that he was. And with this simple yet profound realization, he shifted his mindset completely, no longer perceiving himself as a sick person, but rather as a happy, healthy and positive young man who loved himself and his life. That's what brought him healing. Now, after nearly seven years, Iulian is cancer-free, enjoying his life and thanking God each day for the miracle he performed through him but also for opening his eyes and helping him see himself and others for who they truly are rather than any limiting label that might narrowly define them.

THE PATH TO "GIVING UP"

1. Your Place Is Not in a "Box"

We believe in a personal, unique, and separate identity—but if we dare to examine it, we find that this identity depends entirely on an endless collection of things to prop it up: our name, our "biography," our partners, family, home, job, friends, credit cards . . . It is on their fragile and transient support that we rely for our security. So when they are all taken away, will we have any idea of who we really are?

Without our familiar props, we are faced with just ourselves, a person we do not know, an unnerving stranger with whom we have been living all the time but we never really wanted to meet. Isn't that why we have tried to fill every moment of time with noise and activity, however boring or trivial, to ensure that we are never left in silence with this stranger on our own?

—SOGYAL RINPOCHE

We live in a world where people are constantly defining boundaries, using all kinds of categorical and stereotypical labels to separate themselves from those around them, and thinking that based on the labels each individual carries, they will know how to treat everyone. And they will know who are the people they should associate with and who are the people they should stay away from.

When you place yourself and the world around you in "boxes," and when you label everyone around you based on how they look, what they do for a living, based on their beliefs, physical appearance, social status, sexual orientation, gender, and so on, and label yourself the same way, you create a huge gap between you and the world around you, between your heart and theirs. You forget that we are all in this together, and you cease to remember that who we are underneath it all has no color, no race and no interest in placing everything and everyone into "boxes" and categories and then treating them all according to the instructions written on those many "boxes."

Most of us were raised to believe that labels are meant to help us become more aware of our value and our own worth, and that they are meant to help us differentiate ourselves from those who are different than us, when in fact, these labels don't really say much about who we truly are, since they only define our actions and our interactions, our behaviors and attitudes, and not our true nature. Just as the map is not the territory, so too the labels you place on people don't actually define who they are.

People, places and experiences aren't meant to be labeled and judged, they are meant to be loved and appreciated, since deep down inside, the nature we all share is love, light and happiness.

2. Labels Deny You the Right to Realize Your True Nature

Once you label me you negate me.

—SØREN KIERKEGAARD

Who we are underneath it all is much grander and much more complex than our conceptual structure of reality, much more precious and a lot more valuable than all the labels that have been placed on us up until this moment, and all the labels that will continue to be placed on us in the future.

Our true nature is fluid and expansive, constantly growing and constantly expanding. And when we use all kinds of rigid concepts and labels to define ourselves, conforming to strict ideas of who we are, we deny ourselves the right to realize our true nature. We deny ourselves the right to be the unique, powerful and loving beings we were born to be. And instead of continuing to be supple as a newborn child, and instead of remaining soft and flexible like water, we become hard and rigid, living our lives from a place of doubt, fear and limitation and continuing to perceive ourselves as being more or less valuable than those around us based on the labels we all carry.

There is so much more to each and every one of us than our name, our past, our partners, family, friends, job, material possessions, and the many categorical and stereotypical labels that the world around us has placed on us. And it's only by giving up the need to constantly label ourselves, our experiences, our lives and the lives of those around us that we can fully experience and understand this truth.

3. Focus on the Depth More Than the Surface

> Do not hover always on the surface of things, nor take up suddenly with mere appearances; but penetrate into the depth of matters, as far as your time and circumstances allow.
>
> —ISAAC WATTS

Put down your label maker and dare to look at the deeper meaning of things. Look beyond the surface. Look deep into people's hearts and look deep into your own soul.

Look at everything with curiosity, with love and compassion. Understand that there is more to life than what meets the eye. There is more to people, places, experiences and things than what you see at first glance.

Focus on the depth more than the surface; focus on the beauty and the light that is hidden in each and every one of us and less on the darkness.

Seek to understand why things are the way they are, why people behave the way they do, and why you are experiencing the things you are experiencing. Keep an open mind and try to understand the whole of life, not just one small part of it.

4. We Are All in This Together

No man is an island, entire of itself; every man is a piece of the continent, a part of the main. If a cloud be washed away by the sea, Europe is the less, as well as if a promontory were, as well as if a manor of thy friend's or of thine own were: any man's death diminishes me, because I am involved in mankind, and therefore never send to know for whom the bells tolls; it tolls for thee.

—JOHN DONNE

It's true that we live in a world where labels need to be used so that we won't have chaos and madness present all around us. And it's true that many of the labels we use are meant to help us manage and guide our conduct, to navigate the many decisions we have to make and to contribute to a clear and healthy communication between us. But it's also true that labels are often meant to divide us from one another, creating a false sense of separation between us, causing us to perceive some people as being more important and more valuable than others.

We are all in this together. This planet belongs to all of us, and there isn't one human being on this earth who is more deserving than another.

We are all equally valuable and equally important. Even though some of us might be more knowledgeable than others, and even though some people might lead better and richer lives than others do, it doesn't mean that those people are more important, more superior or more deserving. It only means that they have lived under different circumstances than others have and that they were shaped differently than others were.

So give up labels and make no distinction between people based on age, sex, social status, color, religion or race. Seek to live your life believing in the equality of all.

Chapter 15

GIVE UP ATTACHMENT

In the end these things matter most: How well did you love? How fully did you live? How deeply did you let go?

—BUDDHA

MY STORY

I think it's time for me to leave Mindvalley, I remember thinking to myself one morning as I was preparing to go to work.

On some level, it felt crazy for me to want to leave behind the great life I was living, all the people I loved, my job, the regular paradise island vacations, and the work I was doing at Mindvalley. And so I decided to ignore those "irrational" thoughts and what my heart and intuition were asking me to do, hoping that by doing so, I would silence their voice in the end.

However, the more I tried to silence my inner voice and ignore the many signals and messages that my heart and intuition were sending my way, the more restless I began to feel and the more aggressively my body seemed to react to what I was doing.

I got sick that year like I had never been sick in my whole life, and I had days when I literally couldn't get up from my bed to go to work, crying my eyes out and fearing that I would get fired for being sick all the time.

"Get up! Move!" I kept telling myself one morning after being in bed for almost one week.

"Please get up! You have to go to work! You'll soon get fired if you don't!"

But my body didn't want to move. It no longer wanted to listen to me. And I knew that things were only going to get worse and worse if I continued to pretend that I didn't know what was causing me all that pain, sickness, anger and unhappiness.

I was in denial for months, not wanting to face the truth, thinking that if I let go of my attachment to all the things I so much loved, I was going to go back to feeling unhappy, unworthy and unloved. I was going to lose everything, and I was going to go back to living a life that had no purpose and no meaning.

I tried very hard to keep life from taking its natural course, hoping that by clinging to everything and everyone, I was going to be allowed to keep all those people, places and experiences forever in my life. What I failed to realize was that I was no longer happy and that I was already feeling alone, lost, unloved and unworthy. I was already living a life that no longer had purpose, that no longer had meaning. And I was already losing everything by trying to cling to everything.

. . .

"Vishen, I think it's time for me to leave Mindvalley," I said one day during our lunch together.

"I've been trying very hard to keep this from happening, but for some reason unknown to me, my heart and intuition are asking me to leave the life I have here and start a new life someplace else.

"I love this place and I don't want to leave. It makes no sense to my rational mind, but I am tired of trying to resist. I just know that I am being called to leave and move on to the next chapter."

By the time I finished telling him all that I had to say, a great sense of inner peace had enveloped me, and all of a sudden I felt as if a heavy burden had been lifted from my heart. And in that moment I knew that I had done the right thing.

Little did I know that the next chapter involved me returning to Romania to complete this book, and to make peace with the tragic childhood memories of my upbringing, so that I could find deeper happiness and fulfillment.

LESSONS IN LETTING GO

As human beings we all want to be happy and free from misery . . . we have learned that the key to happiness is inner peace. The greatest obstacles to inner peace are disturbing emotions such as anger, attachment, fear and suspicion, while love and compassion and a sense of universal responsibility are the sources of peace and happiness.

—DALAI LAMA

Having had a very unhappy upbringing, I thought I was supposed to cling to all those things, people, places and experiences that made me feel happy and loved. I thought it was my job to hold on to them because if I didn't I was going to lose everything and go back to feeling lost, unloved and unhappy. And the moment life "forced" me to surrender, to give up my attachment and to trust that if I did so life would take even better care of me, that was the moment I realized that happiness will never come from holding on to things, but only from letting them go.

Simona, a friend and neighbor of mine, knows about this all too well. After the death of her newborn son, Simona fell into a deep depression. The memory of her walking back home from the hospital without her little boy in her arms drove her very close to the edge. Her health started deteriorating, her marriage began to fall apart, and her will to live was almost gone. She couldn't think of anything else except her little boy who never got to receive the love and affection of his parents. Simona was eventually able to let go when she realized that her attachment was poisoning all areas of her life, interfering not only with the love she had for her lost child, but also with the love she had for herself, her husband and for life itself. This shift in perception helped heal many of her wounds. It filled her heart with love, and it also brought a lot of light and peace to all those places where there had once been so much pain and darkness.

Letting it all go was the best decision she could make, and it was an eye-opening experience for Simona, and for her husband as well. It was almost as if they rediscovered themselves and fell back in love, after a very stormy and dark period. The love for their baby was still there, in their hearts, but they decided to live in the present and not let that loss define the rest of their lives.

Everything in life changes. Nothing stays the same. And the more you try to cling to things, desperately trying to control and change the natural course of life, the more you will suffer and the unhappier your life will get.

When you hold on too tightly to everything and everyone, when you desperately try to cling to things, people, places and experiences, you take the life out of them and you keep life from taking you where you need to go.

Happiness can never come from attachment to transitory things. It can only come from letting go. Freedom can never come from clinging. It can only come from giving up attachment.

THE PATH TO "GIVING UP"

1. Nothing in Life Is Yours to Keep

All of our miseries are nothing but attachment. Our whole ignorance and darkness is a strange combination of a thousand and one attachments. And we are attached to things which will be taken away by the time of death, or even perhaps before. You may be very much attached to money but you can go bankrupt tomorrow. You may be very much attached to your power and position, your presidency, your prime ministership, but they are like soap bubbles. Today they are here, tomorrow not even a trace will be left.

—OSHO

Nothing in life is yours to keep—not your children, not your friends and family, not your lover, not your material possessions, not your youth and vitality, not your struggles (which is great news) or successes, not your body and not even your life. Everything in life is given to you for a short period of time, to enjoy, to learn from, to appreciate and to love, but never to keep.

Things, people, and experiences all come and go. Everything changes, nothing remains the same, and the more you resist this truth, the more you try to control the natural course of life by clinging to transitory things, the more complicated your life will get and the more you will continue to suffer.

People try to hold on to life because they fear dying. But learning to live isn't about grasping on to things. It isn't about clinging to everything and everyone. It's about learning to let go.

Learning to live is learning to let go. Learning to let go is learning to be happy.

Learning to live is learning to let go.

Let go of your attachment to your past, to those you love, to your material possessions, to your ideas, thoughts and feelings, and allow yourself to be free.

Bring a final end to your clinging. Bring a final end to your suffering. Awaken from the ignorance you have been living in for so long and accept life as it is. Know that, as Bodhidharma put it, "Once you stop clinging and let things be, you'll be free, even of birth and death. You'll transform everything."

2. Contemplate Deeply on the Truth of Impermanence

What is born will die, What has been gathered will be dispersed, What has been accumulated will be exhausted, What has been built up will collapse, And what has been high will be brought low.

—SOGYAL RINPOCHE

Reflect on the transitory nature of life. Remind yourself that nothing in this life is yours to keep, that everything in life has a beginning and an end, that nothing lasts forever and that eventually everything fades away. Remind yourself as often as possible that happiness can never be found in clinging, that it can only be found in letting go.

Look outside in nature for evidence of decay, destruction, death, rebirth, rejuvenation and renewal. And remind yourself that you too are part of nature. That you too are going through these natural stages.

Allow nature to be your wise friend, teacher and trusted companion. Allow nature to heal and comfort you, to teach you more about the infinite circle of life, about life, about love and about letting go. Adopt the pace of nature. Do what nature does. Live like nature lives.

Reflect on your mortality and on everyone else's mortality, no matter how cold and morbid that might seem, and know that doing this will help you let go of your attachments and it will help you make peace with your mortality. This is when you start to fully live your life. Because just as Elisabeth Kübler-Ross said, "It is only when we truly know and understand that we have a limited time on Earth and that we have no way of knowing when our time is up that we will begin to live each day to the fullest, as if it were the only one we had."

Contemplate deeply on the impermanence of things, and when you do so your whole life will forever change, for the better.

3. Release All Grasping and Relax into Your True Nature

He who knows me as his own divine Self breaks through the belief that he is the body and is not reborn as a separate creature. Such a one is united with me. Delivered from selfish attachment, fear, and anger, filled with me, surrendering themselves to me, purified in the fire of my being, many have reached the state of unity in me.

—BHAGAVAD GITA

You are the main character in the story of your life, just like everyone else is the main character in their own story. And the relationship you have with your true self, with your inner divinity and with the source of all things should be the most important relationship in your life. Just as it should be the most important relationship in everyone else's life. Why?

Because only by honoring ourselves and only by living our lives from a place of truth, honesty and integrity can we be of service to one another, and only by being true to ourselves can we be true to one another.

In the New Testament this idea is portrayed so beautifully: "He that loves father or mother more than me is not worthy of me, and he that loves son or daughter more than me is not worthy of me" (Matthew 10:37). In *The Prophet* by Khalil Gibran as well: "Your children are not your children. They are the sons and daughters of Life's longing for itself. They came through you but not from you and though they are with you yet they belong not to you."

We are all here for a reason. Each and every one of us has a purpose to fulfill. And that purpose and that reason isn't about clinging to transitory things; it isn't about getting attached to people, places and experiences and then using them as an excuse for why we can't live the life we are meant to live.

You may be a parent, you may be a wife or a husband, a friend, a sister or a brother . . . and even though it's natural to love and care for those close to you and want the best for them, the important thing is to never cling to anyone, to never act as if you possess those around you, to never interfere with who they are and the path they need to walk on, and to never allow them to interfere with who you are. Never allow the "obligations" of being in a relationship with the people in your life to stand in the way of who you truly are, or in the way of doing the work that your soul came here to do.

Give up attachment and allow yourself and everyone around you to live the life they are meant to live. Don't play God with anyone. Know that just as you have your own unique path to walk on, so does everyone else.

Release all grasping and relax into your true nature.

4. Love Everything, Be Attached to Nothing

Pleasure in its fullness, cannot be experienced when one is grasping it. I knew a little girl to whom someone gave a bunny rabbit. She was so delighted with the bunny rabbit and so afraid of losing it, that taking it home in the car, she squeezed it to death with love. And lots of parents do that to their children. And lots of spouses do it to each other. They hold on too hard, and so take the life out of this transient, beautifully fragile thing that life is . . . To have it, to have life, and to have its pleasure, you must at the same time let go of it.

—ALAN WATTS

Many people confuse their clingy, fearful and possessive behavior with love, failing to realize that love and attachment have nothing to do with each other. Attachment comes from a place of fear—fear of losing everything you have; fear of not being able to re-create the life you are currently living; fear of losing the love of those close to you, fear of losing your social status, your wealth and material possessions, fear of dying, and so on, while love . . . well, real love is pure and kind, and its only interest is in loving.

Love has no interest in clinging, possessing or in keeping the people in our lives bound to us. Love only wants to love.

Love yourself. Love your life, your children, your spouse, your friends, your work and your living environment. Love and appreciate the many things, people and experiences that life sends your way, but don't try to cling to them. Keep yourself, your relationships and your whole life free from bondage, and when the time comes to let go, when life asks you to let go, do so with grace.

Give up all your attachments and allow love to free you

from the self-made prison you have been living in for so long. Allow love to run through every cell of your body and to govern all areas of your life.

Let love teach you that happiness will never come from possessing, from clinging or from holding on to impermanence, but only from letting go.

Let go of attachment and allow yourself to become one with love. Because love is who you are. Love is what you are made of—and what you are made for.

FINAL NOTE

Your task is not to seek for love, but merely to seek and find all the barriers within yourself that you have built against it.

—RUMI

It was a beautiful sunny day. My father noticed the curious desire in my eyes as we walked back home.

"You'd like an ice cream, wouldn't you?" my father asked a much younger me back then, with a rare smile on his face.

"Give this little kid an ice cream," he told the ice-cream lady. *"This little girl deserves one."*

That is the only pleasant vivid memory I have of him, the only time I clearly witnessed him allowing his inner light to shine. And that is what's both strange and beautiful about our human nature.

Even though all throughout my childhood years I got ridiculed, labeled, judged and laughed at constantly, and even though I suffered tremendously because of my father's lack of love, his abusive and toxic behavior, I managed to find the inner strength, wisdom and courage to carve through the rough walls that had been imprisoning the real me for all of those years and free myself from the dark, cold and fearful world I was living in.

Instead of continuing to cling to all those traumatic and painful memories, taking my sense of worth from all the wrong places, and instead of allowing the darkness of the past to poison my mind, my heart and my life, I decided to give it all up. I decided to give up my attachment to all those toxic thoughts, attitudes, relationships and behaviors that were holding me back. I decided to die to the past so that I could be born again to the present. No longer fighting, rejecting and resisting what was, but rather accepting, releasing, forgiving and making peace with it all.

As I have mentioned throughout this book, deep down inside our true nature is love. But as we grow older, bit by bit, our true nature becomes buried under layers of societal conditioning. As a result, we start experiencing our lives through the filters of the many fearful and limiting beliefs we adopt from those around us.

We perceive ourselves as being small, powerless, alone and insignificant when in fact we are powerful beyond measure.

It's never too late to start all over. It's never too late to claim your right to life and to happiness. No matter where you've been, no matter how life treated you in the past and no matter how many times you were hurt and injured mentally, emotionally or physically, if you're still here, you can begin again.

Fill your heart with love. Forgive and let go.

Give up and be happy!

ACKNOWLEDGMENTS

So many people have supported and encouraged me through this wonderful journey of writing my first book. And I would like to specifically thank:

God and my soul for helping me bring so much light, love and truth into my life.

My mom for passing her gift of writing to me and my father for being my greatest teacher.

Amir Ahmad, for helping me believe in myself as much as he himself believed in me and for pushing me to write this book. Amir, through everything you said and through everything you did for me, you helped me find the inner strength, the courage and the confidence I needed to heal my wounds, to make peace with my past and to share my story with the rest of the world.

The Mindvalley community and Vishen Lakhiani, the founder of Mindvalley, for bringing such an amazing group of people together.

My friends and family for all their help and support.

The readers of PurposeFairy blog, for walking this wonderful and magical journey with me.

My editor, Marian Lizzi, for being patient with me and for taking my draft and suggesting such great improvements that I've now turned it into this book.

FURTHER READING

Tao Te Ching by Lao Tzu, Stephen Mitchell translation

Excuses Begone! by Wayne W. Dyer

A Complaint Free World: How to Stop Complaining and Start Enjoying the Life You Always Wanted by Will Bowen

You Can Heal Your Life by Louise Hay

The Power of Now by Eckhart Tolle

A Return to Love: Reflections on the Principles of "A Course in Miracles" by Marianne Williamson

Love: What Life Is All About by Leo F. Buscaglia

ABOUT THE AUTHOR

Mate Valtr

Luminita D. Saviuc is the playful spirit behind the popular PurposeFairy blog. She was born and raised in Romania, but since then has lived in many countries around the world in search of Self and Soul. Her acclaimed blog post, "15 Things You Should Give Up To Be Happy," was shared by over 1.2 million people on Facebook and later became the heart of this book. Through everything she is and everything she does, Luminita continues her work of shining light in the world. She is writing, speaking, and creating new ways to share her inspiring message of self-empowerment.